A SHORT HISTORY OF *CAHIERS DU CINÉMA*

A SHORT HISTORY OF *CAHIERS DU CINÉMA*

Emilie Bickerton

VERSO
London • New York

First published by Verso 2009

1 3 5 7 9 10 8 6 4 2

Verso
UK: 6 Meard Street, London W1F 0EG
US: 20 Jay Street, Suite 1010, Brooklyn, NY 11201
www.versobooks.com

Verso is the imprint of New Left Books

ISBN-13: 978-1-84467-232-5

British Library Cataloguing in Publication Data
A catalogue record for this book is available from the British Library

Library of Congress Cataloging-in-Publication Data
A catalog record for this book is available from the Library of Congress

Typeset by Hewer Text UK Ltd, Edinburgh
Printed by in the US by Maple Vail

Contents

Acknowledgements

I would like to thank my colleagues at *New Left Review*, in particular Susan Watkins, Tony Wood and Perry Anderson for their comments on earlier versions of this book. Johanna Zhang for the pictures—technically, conceptually—and our walks and talks where much of what follows became a little clearer. And thank you to all those who helped and advised me in different but invaluable ways: Christopher Bickerton, Sebastian Budgen, Tom Penn, Lorna Scott Fox, Michael Witt, Emma Wilson, Julien Planté, Laura Mulvey, Adam Shatz, Patrick Hayes. In Paris, many of those who lived the *Cahiers* story were kind enough to share their memories with me. Their time and gift for recounting such a remarkable tale allowed me to better understand the lived experience of writing for the journal. In particular, thank you: Raymond Bellour, Jean-Louis Comolli, Jean Douchet, Bernard Eisenschitz, Jean-André Fieschi, André S. Labarthe and Sylvie Pierre. For my family, as ever, my deepest gratitude: Hélene and David, Claire, Paul and Chris.

Charles Laughton, *Night of the Hunter* (1955)

Introduction

What follows is a familiar tale, and yet it has never been told. In its original conception the French film journal *Cahiers du cinéma* had marked a break with the prevailing regimes of taste in the artistic culture of the post-war. In film this was defined by the silent tradition and French *cinéma de qualité*—glossy literary adaptations, costume dramas or musicals—both unanimously celebrated for reasons motivated by patriotism or partisanship. *Cahiers* proposed a very different notion of cinema and turned consensus opinion on its head. Its writers believed that film was not only an entertainment industry but also an art at the beginning of its journey. Film had already produced a number of great masters, equal to Velázquez or Proust in their field. In the writing on film however, there was too much nostalgia for a bygone era. Old-guard critics were shut away in their decrepit palaces, cut off from the world like Billy Wilder's fallen movie star in *Sunset Boulevard*. In the first issue *Cahiers* put it simply: this group of critics were 'lovers of a dead sun, they see ashes where a thousand phoenix are constantly reborn'.[1]

It was the last modernist project. As Jean-Luc Godard summed up in 1959:

> We have won by getting the principle accepted that a film by Hitchcock is as important as a book by Aragon. The *auteurs* of films, thanks to us, have entered definitively into the history of art.[2]

1 François Chalais, *Cahiers* 1, April 1951.
2 Jean-Luc Godard, *Arts*, 22 April 1959.

Bound in its original yellow covers, *Cahiers* was a real *journal de combat*—a magazine with a battle plan. It drew its polemical energy from the remarkable combination of individuals who made up its first editorial group. This eclectic team brought a mixture of Catholicism, classicism, humanism and metaphysics to the meeting with cinema. Born in a growing Cold War climate where public figures and debates were positioned vis-à-vis an emerging world order, *Cahiers* initially set itself apart. It focused on developing a deeper engagement with cinema built on aesthetic foundations. Such a rich body of work was in need of fuller understanding: at home there was Jean Renoir, and early pioneers Jean Vigo and Jean Epstein; the cinematographic landscape worldwide included Italian neo-realism through Roberto Rossellini and Luchino Visconti; in America the exiles Fritz Lang and Alfred Hitchcock worked alongside Samuel Fuller, Nicholas Ray and Billy Wilder; Yasujiro Ozu, Akira Kurosawa, Kenji Mizoguchi were active to the East. Such directors had to be defended in a coherent fashion, within the context of the history of art.

The process of viewing the films by these masters also provided *Cahiers* critics with an education in how to make films. The young Turks, as Claude Chabrol, Jean-Luc Godard, François Truffaut, Jacques Rivette and Eric Rohmer became known, were preparing their own practical intervention into the world of cinema, in which the journal was the first stage. *Cahiers* was their 'rancho notorious' in one former editor's phrase, evoking Fritz Lang's hideaway for outlaws, a gathering place where the young men—until Sylvie Pierre's arrival in the sixties, no women worked at *Cahiers*—could explore and find ways to articulate the genius they had seen in films. Here they could live and breathe the movies, argue and debate over the latest screening, find the right words to justify their passions and, crucially, meet some of the masters. Writing forced them to ask, and answer, how a director employed various techniques to his own unique ends, how he conveyed his narrative visually and developed a thematic continuity through his œuvre. The years 1951–1959 were explosive ones for *Cahiers*, concluding triumphantly when François Truffaut collected the Palme d'Or at Cannes. Having previously dismissed or denied the critical and now artistic radicalism coming from the magazine's pages, critics internationally could only eat their words.

Up to this point, the story of the journal is broadly well known. These were the iconic 'yellow years', when some angry young men first cut their teeth before enacting the short-lived cinematic revolution of the New Wave. A few moments have become emblematic, and suffice to sum up this version of the magazine's history. A young Jean-Pierre Léaud's defiant stare at the camera in *The 400 Blows*; the jump cuts between Jean-Paul Belmondo and Jean Seberg walking down the Champs-Elysées in *Breathless*; Miles Davis's jazz score narrating Louis Malle's drama in an elevator, *Lift to the Scaffold*. These moments punctured the previous conception of what cinema could express and how. Suddenly the conventional studio settings, tight scenarios and rules of editing were replaced with low-budget techniques and audacious working methods. Small teams shot scenes on the streets and in friends' apartments with mobile cameras and using direct sound; takes and tracking shots grew unusually long; experiments with editing led to the use of collage and jump cuts; the love affair with America brought in jazz and William Faulkner. The ethnographic *cinéma vérité* practiced by Jean Rouch and Robert Flaherty met with *noir* plot lines full of guns, women and motor cars. But for all the eulogies that have subsequently been devoted to the New Wave, the movement was brief, over by 1965. Its influence was absolutely definitive, but the work itself was insubstantial. The ideas developed at *Cahiers* during its first ten years also faced the challenge of moving on from its first success to grasp a transformed cinematic landscape in the sixties.

Cahiers managed to build on the New Wave and redefined itself on successive occasions throughout the sixties and seventies, generating consistently radical critical writing and ideas on film. In these decades the periodic renewals of the editorial team led to greater internationalism, some of the earliest applications of structuralism and psychoanalysis to film, politicized and ideological critiques that turned the gaze on the spectator, and considerations around the impact of television on the moving image. The major flashpoints that distilled the defining questions involved both personalities and outside events.

In the sixties, the clash between Rivette and Rohmer was really a conflict over their world view. As editor from 1959, Rohmer retained the classical cinephile tastes developed during *Cahiers*' first ten years, staying faithful to a more timeless approach and maintaining his devotion to the old masters. For Rivette, this critical position was impotent in the face of modern cinema. Concentrating on a director's choice of the cinematic presentation of a story could not fully explain the work being produced by Pier Paolo Pasolini, Glauber Rocha or Nagasi Oshima. More instructive were the ideas of Lévi-Strauss, the music of Pierre Boulez and the abstract canvases of Mark Rothko.

In the seventies it was not just the world of art and ideas that *Cahiers* turned towards, but also politics. The glorious isolation of the artist and critic was rigorously re-appraised. *Cahiers*' 'red years', which involved a brief lurch into Maoism, are its most notorious. It is a decade marked by varying degrees of ideological intransigence, artistic austerity and auto-critique. Among the debris of a defeated revolutionary fervour, *Cahiers* stepped back in 1974 to reconsider its critical function. The texts that were produced during these tumultuous years are now the most widely translated in *Cahiers*' archive, and are cornerstones for contemporary film theory. The discordance that eventually defined the new direction for the magazine in the eighties involved Serge Toubiana (who first arrived as a Red Book-waving Maoist) and Serge Daney. Toubiana would eventually push through his more 'connected', glossy and up-market vision for *Cahiers*, eclipsing Daney's less clearly defined, more exploratory and critically radical alternative. The consequence of this split is still in evidence today: the eighties was the decade when *Cahiers* joined the ruck of mainstream cinema guides preoccupied with Oscar contenders and sales figures, rather than with drawing up battle plans to challenge this market-driven model of film criticism which it has itself become.

Chronology naturally organizes the narrative for the history of any journal. Alongside this, a set of questions and relationships emerge that are at the heart of the *Cahiers* tale, recurring and animating successive generations of editors at the magazine. One is the relationship between art and politics. The positions taken by editors vis-à-vis directors such as Howard Hawks, Hitchcock or Otto

Preminger were possible partly because of the young Turks' lack of politics—they saw the brilliance of the art and did not care about any political narratives that might also exist in the work. They embraced Hollywood for its artistic achievements, in contrast to the anti-Americanism espoused by the Communist Party (which chose Soviet cinema) or French patriots (who fawned over *cinéma de qualité*). This strictly aesthetic project enabled *Cahiers* critics to see artistry in the most apparently ordinary melodrama or formulaic *film noir*. They were looking at everything inside the frame, alert to glimpses of individual and personal brilliance that would sneak through the cracks and tell them that this apparently conventional western could *only* be the work of Anthony Mann or Budd Boetticher.

Cahiers was consciously apolitical so as to avoid the pitfalls of those contributing to *L'Ecran Français*, the Communist Party's *Les Lettres Françaises*, or the left-leaning *Positif*. In these pages, often echoed in American magazines, critics expressed their views about the world through films. When Georges Sadoul saw *Pickup on South Street* at the Venice festival in 1953 he called Fuller 'the McCarthy of cinema'.[3] Yet the same film was deemed outrageously anti-American in the States for its perceived red sympathies. On both sides of the Atlantic this was an example of cinema being viewed for the story alone; no critic, as those at *Cahiers* were wont to do, looked at what the pictures were saying.

The role played by the United States, its influence culturally and its impact and presence politically, has been a vital and defining factor for *Cahiers*. At every stage, its position has been oriented for or against the cinema emerging from that country. In the immediate post-Liberation years before the Cold War set in, America was broadly perceived in France with a mixture of fascination and uncertainty. But for *Cahiers*, it represented the promise of modernity—aesthetic and technological—after the impoverishment suffered during the war, as well as a distinct break from the fight against fascism. Both Jean-

3 Georges Sadoul, letter to Jacques Doniol-Valcroze, 25 September 1955, reproduced in Antoine de Baecque, *La Cinéphilie: Invention d'un regard, histoire d'une culture, 1944–1968*, Paris 2003, p. 178.

Paul Sartre and Simone de Beauvoir would recount the mixture of romance and intrigue America evoked during their trips in the early fifties. *Cahiers* single-handedly elevated aspects of American culture, disregarded in the states as mere entertainment, to the level of art through a process similar to Sartre's appraisals of Faulkner and John Dos Passos. Both these writers, and directors such as Hawks and Hitchcock, were canonized first in France. It was an admiration that long confused critics and audiences internationally, who dismissed many of these cultural products as bubblegum or trash. Even in the eighties there were still signs that this critical astuteness continued: Fuller's *White Dog*—a parable of racism in eighties America—was an end-of-career masterpiece, but it was mostly ignored in the States. The film was widely released and critically celebrated in France.[4]

The Franco-American love affair turned bitter in the late sixties, and this shift was registered by the increasing internationalism of *Cahiers*. Jean-Luc Godard dedicated his first picture to Monogram films and proudly cast Fuller in *Pierrot le fou* and Eddie Constantine in *Alphaville*, but by 1972 it was his cynicism—to make a movie you need a chequebook and stars—that led him to cast Jane Fonda and Yves Montand as leads in *Tout va bien*. Jacques Tati's œuvre captures the progressive evolution from curiosity and excitement to disappointment, disillusion and eventual resistance towards America. The postman François in *Jour de fête*, made at the end of the forties, betrayed exasperated admiration in his attempts to emulate the efficiency of the American mailman that so impressed the locals. *Monsieur Hulot's Holiday* a few years later expressed more scepticism. Tati's protagonist found the rigours involved in 'leisure' impossible to follow, disrupting the regimented holiday routines with his very different conception of freedom and time. Defeat looms in *My Uncle*—even more so in *Playtime* made in 1967. By this point the American lifestyle had set root in France, and Monsieur Hulot's spirit was drained by his foiled attempts to navigate through faceless offices, doors leading nowhere and identical buildings lining streets full of people wearing the same suits and skirts.

4 Serge Daney, *Libération*, 9 July 1982.

To an extent all French cinema, and certainly the generations at *Cahiers*, registered this fluctuating and tense attraction–repulsion towards America, its films, culture and the model for living it exported. During the eighties the editors announced a return to the US after the ties had been severed under the Althusserian and Maoist influence during the red years. Steven Spielberg, George Lucas and Francis Ford Coppola were hailed as a new generation of Hollywood artists. The process and rationale behind this reconciliation was of a very different order, however. The specifically aesthetic and modernist project that had led critics to the early masters working in the studio system was replaced by a model emptied of all its radical content and filled instead with mainstream opinion. The challenge with new Hollywood was thus to talk about *Jaws* and *E.T.*, or later *Fight Club* and *Million Dollar Baby*, in a loftier register than the average movie magazine, but with essentially the same message—don't miss the latest release.

This was presented at the time as *Cahiers* going back to its roots, and also reconnecting the popular base of cinema with the elite practice of cinephilia. This balance between broad appeal and elitism also runs constantly through the *Cahiers* years. Its founding editor and intellectual inspiration, André Bazin, had remarked in 1948 that the two coexisted when the art was born:

> Being destined to appeal to a very wide audience is both the weighty burden and the unique opportunity of cinema. Whereas the output of traditional art forms has evolved, ever since the Renaissance, for the benefit of a small and privileged elite, cinema, by its very nature, is destined to serve the masses all over the world. Any attempt to create an aesthetic from the perspective of a narrow audience is, in the first place, historically inexact and doomed to fail: it leads us up the garden path.[5]

The original avant-garde, from Georges Méliès and D.W. Griffith to Louis Feuillade and Erich von Stroheim, always aimed to make

5 André Bazin, 'Défense de l'avant-garde', *L'Ecran français*, 21 December 1948.

commercial films and aspired to have their works screened to the largest possible audience. In similar spirit, *Cahiers* first championed the films it believed were the best of the art, with the aim to bring a deeper understanding of their value to the wider public, whom it believed perfectly capable of grasping them. Today, the aesthetic choices dictating critical activity and the belief in the capacity of the public to learn and develop have both gone from *Cahiers*.

Writing on popular culture in a higher register, but without the critical project to justify it, also reflects the establishment of film studies as an academic discipline. In its original incarnation, though, *Cahiers* was resolutely anti-establishment, a stance which included antagonism towards the university—the first generation of cinephiles got their education at the movies, not at school. 'I failed my baccalaureate because of Fritz Lang', explained one contributor, Jean-Claude Biette. The idea of studying film within an institution was risible. By the mid-seventies, however, taking film seriously had gone all the way to the academy, and many of *Cahiers*' own texts were on students' reading lists. This has encouraged the separation between criticism as transmission and dissemination and criticism as specialization in its own right. *Cahiers* has flirted with both throughout its history.

The young Turks had always thought of themselves as future directors. The relationship between critic and practitioner has also been an integral factor in *Cahiers*' evolution, yet two of its most influential editors, André Bazin and Serge Daney, did not make the transition. The mixture has always been complex and volatile: the critic–*cinéaste* gave the journal its urgency and demanded an obsessive relationship to cinema; the critic–critic elaborated the intellectual environment within which this obsession could signify. 'I am not a visionary', Daney explained. 'I always needed to be shown, but as soon as a frame exists, I'm very sharp.'[6] Those who show in words and pictures, and those who work exclusively by watching—the history of *Cahiers* reveals how art and its criticism requires both.

The cinematic landscape itself explains the *Cahiers* story up to a point. Without Italian neo-realism, without the suspense of

6 Serge Daney, *Persévérance*, Paris 2003, p. 124.

Hitchcock, the screwball comedies of Hawks or the saturated melodramas of Douglas Sirk, what would the Young Turks have rallied around? If there had been no Jean Renoir or Orson Welles, who would have shown André Bazin that cinema was an impure art that could, in its very structure or montage, also bring us the deepest insights into reality? It was because Michelangelo Antonioni, Rocha and John Cassavetes existed that Rivette had to break with a pure *mise en scène* approach if he wanted to make sense of their work.

Cinema is of course the vital ingredient in *Cahiers*' history, and what constitutes modern cinema has always been the driving force of its investigations. This has often made the journal's projects visionary—seeing cinema where others saw cheap nonsense, or nothing at all; but also responsive—given the nature of cinema as it is being made, what is to be done? Along the way there have been various priorities: the destruction of prevailing value systems and the elevation of the *film maudit*; the creation of a canon via concepts unique to cinema, and the application of approaches to what it means to be human, from metaphysics to structuralism; taking into account the spectator's particular position within this system of meaning and politicizing the very act of film criticism.

Yet in turn, what would neo-realism have been without Bazin; Hitchcock without Truffaut; Ray without Godard? At *Cahiers*, for the first time, cinema was reflected upon and writers nourished a discussion around it, creating a culture that could receive it. The pronouncements they made not only shaped the journal's particular history, but also sketched out a grand narrative for film.

The history of *Cahiers* is moulded by remarkable individuals, but their mark has been so powerful only because there was a collective project uniting various generations of editors. Bazin played a key diplomatic role in the treacherous years when the journal had no glorious tradition to prop it up. He balanced the polemical with the gracious, using his own cachet as an established writer and animator to lend legitimacy to the shocking statements flung out by the petulant young Turks; he battled hard to maintain friendship with Sadoul, aware of the critic's influence in Paris at the time. Bazin's lifetime and that of *Cahiers* coincided for only seven years, but his thought has nourished its pages to this day, not to mention those of other journals, and other theorists of cinema. Truffaut transformed the interview into a critical tool; with his anti-authoritarian nature he was devastating in his attack on the dominant French cinema of the time. Rivette's particularly passionate reaction after a film screening marked every editor in his presence. His clash with Rohmer crystallized the tensions between classicism and modernism that cinema faced entering the sixties. Godard's trajectory helps to explain *Cahiers*' own flirtations with Maoism, militancy and explorations of various multimedia. Daney would be the last to lead the critical function in a new and vanguard direction.

This book tells the story of what happened to the world's most important film magazine—how such a project as *Cahiers* was possible, why it emerged in France rather than elsewhere, and the reasons it eventually came to an end; limping on today as just another banal mouthpiece for the spectacle. It is a history of seeing and learning how to see. 'We were all Hegelians', Eric Rohmer has explained retrospectively. 'We believed the judgements we were making on films were historical ones.' And they were. *Cahiers* is partly responsible for writing the history of cinema in the twentieth century. Without it, and its immortal archive, those pictures would certainly mean less to us today.

Billy Wilder, *Sunset Boulevard* (1950)

1

The Crucible

In April 1951 a slim yellow-covered journal, *Cahiers du cinéma, Revue mensuelle du cinéma et du télécinéma*, was published from a cramped room at 146, avenue des Champs-Elysées. Its opening manifesto denounced 'the malevolent neutralism that would tolerate a mediocre cinema, a prudential criticism and a stupefied public'. The prevailing value judgements around film by French critics and audiences, based on political persuasions, driven by patriotic impulses and the lazy assumption that film was an impoverished extension of theatre or literature rather than an art in its own right, were to be demolished once and for all. Cited as examples of the cinema the new journal would champion were Robert Bresson's *Diary of a Country Priest*, Edward Dmytryk's *Give Us This Day*, Billy Wilder's *Sunset Boulevard* and Vittorio de Sica's *Miracle in Milan*—all then on recent release in Paris. The project that had been set in motion made history. When a group including André Bazin, Claude Chabrol, Jean-Luc Godard, Jacques Rivette, Eric Rohmer and François Truffaut combined to form the first editorial team, they had mountains to climb. The proposition that the movies, and especially those westerns, *noirs* and melodramas from Hollywood, could be art was preposterous in the mid-twentieth century. But *Cahiers* wanted to write about Samuel Fuller as if he were Christopher Marlowe, or compare Roberto Rossellini to Henri Matisse, because they were all artists, and belonged to the same world. Film directors were the equals of any great novelist or painter.

Cahiers initiated the final modernist project, as a magazine with the aim of consecrating cinema to the realm of the arts. By 1959 it had succeeded. The denouement is disappointing, but *Cahiers*' life cycle is remarkable: from the true *caméra-stylo*, to paraphrase Alexandre Astruc, whose interventions engaged and provoked film-makers into action and helped shape the way cinema was understood and experienced popularly and theoretically, to the consumer guide published today. What gave rise to the birth of this little magazine that would have such an enormous impact? Why in France, and at this time? And after its first glory years, how did the journal develop, and why in such directions? To answer these questions, we must turn first to the years that preceded April 1951 and the environment out of which *Cahiers* emerged.

The first wave

In 1895 the pioneering film-makers Auguste and Louis Lumière had declared that film was an invention with no future, but developments in the medium soon proved them wrong: it was fertile ground for a mix of styles and genres—surrealism, expressionism, naturalism, realism, poetry, gothic horror—and equally so for the interchange between criticism and practice. *Cahiers*' deepest roots lie in the rich experimental work by critics and directors from the pre-war era of silent film and the early talkies. Throughout the twenties and thirties there were passionate debates over the impact of sound, the role of the director or *metteur en scène*, and the possibilities of the camera. The industry itself was vibrant: France had the largest output of any nation in the world up to 1914, contributing 90 per cent of all films distributed internationally. Crisis hit in the 1920s with increasing competition from Hollywood's studios—by 1928, 85 per cent of the films distributed around the world were American—but still the French public forum for screenings and discussions continued to expand dramatically.[1] Writing on cinema was beginning to flourish as well. Almost every Parisian weekly ran a regular review column, quasi-independent film journals were being set up with an array of contributors—Louis Delluc's *Le Film* brought together Aragon,

1 Data from Catherine Fowler, *The European Film Reader*, London 2002, p. 106; David Coward, *A History of French Literature*, Oxford 2002, p. 538.

Colette, Cocteau and L'Herbier—and books devoted to the medium were appearing, with Delluc's *Photogénie* in 1920 and Jean Epstein's *Bonjour Cinéma* a year later among the most original and substantial.

Cine-clubs were a popular outlet for film screenings. These represented a very different distribution and exhibition model to that which existed in the United States, where each of the small number of major production companies owned all the theatres in which its products could be screened. In contrast, most cine-clubs in France were independent ventures, and often run by or associated with avant-garde directors, whose works would be included on the programme. As a result, there was no distinction between popular entertainment pictures and elite art-house. Safe in the knowledge that cine-clubs would provide a venue, experimental films were made with every intention of reaching a large audience. The presciently named Club des Amis du Septième Art was the first cine-club to open its doors, founded in Paris in 1920 by Futurist and art critic Ricciotto Canudo, quickly followed by similar initiatives from Delluc and a number of other active film-makers and critics, including Germaine Dulac, Léon Moussinac and Jean Renoir. Post-screening discussions and the contents of new journals were dominated by aesthetic questions over the cinematic craft and what its unique techniques and attributes were. In some quarters, however, these animated debates had an underlying nationalist spirit. A home-grown director was celebrated for his expression of a distinctively French cinematic style and consequently his confirmation of the country's prestige. The sense of competition from Hollywood spurred this, and it encouraged a deep-seated suspicion of, if not direct opposition to, American films.

The shock of sound

When talking pictures were introduced in 1929, the French claim to lead the world in matters cinematic was directly challenged. No domestically developed sound film recording system had proved commercially viable, allowing American and German–Dutch companies to step in. France was squeezed out of negotiations at a Paris conference addressing the issues in 1930, as other national representatives divided up control of the new technology amongst themselves. In France sound was met with much suspicion from all quarters, including those early defenders of cinema's uniqueness. Because this had been founded on the idea of film as 'pure poetry' of the visible, sound was held to turn it into 'canned theatre'. Most French critics were pessimistic: 'I love cinema deeply', Alexandre Arnoux wrote, capturing in his lament the pervasive mood:

> its interplay of black and white, its silence, its linked rhythms of images, its relegation of speech, that old human bondage, to the background, seem to me the promises of a wonderful art. And now the savage invention has come along to destroy everything.[2]

Walter Benjamin, in Paris during this period, was also concerned by the arrival of sound, but striking a more political note, worried that it might undermine what he believed was the 'revolutionary primacy' of silent film.[3] Jean Epstein was one of the few early defenders, drawing quite the opposite conclusion to Benjamin: sound had the potential to bring about a revolution in its own right. A more mobile camera was already opening some very exciting prospects; directors must strive to 'set the camera free', place it 'in footballs launched in rockets, on the back of a galloping horse, on buoys during the storm; crouch with it in the cellar, take it up to the ceiling heights'. Adding sound to this offered even more heady possibilities: 'let's imagine movements of sound!' The microphone was free to follow the mobile camera or take an independent trajectory. Epstein believed that reality could be transformed through the additional contribution of the audio recorder, as it had been transformed already by the film image.[4]

---

2 Arnoux, 'L'Expression de la peur', *Pour vous*, 2 May 1929.

3 Letter to Adorno, 1938, reprinted in *Aesthetics and Politics*, London 1977, p. 140.

4 'Le Cinématographe continue', *Cinéa-ciné*, 1930, reprinted in Jean Epstein, *Ecrits sur le cinéma*, vol. 1, Paris 1974. For an English translation see Richard Abel, *French Film Theory and Criticism, Volume 2: 1929–1939*, Princeton 1993, pp. 63–6.

The arrival of sound reignited the debate that had been raging in the twenties and thirties over cinema's relationship to theatre, within which we can see some of the elements that would feature at the heart of *Cahiers*' first polemics. At both extremes in the thirties were Marcel Pagnol and René Clair, two popular directors who locked horns over the definition of their role. For Pagnol, there was no artistic creation involved in making a film. Cinema was a 'minor art' that merely recorded and disseminated existing works (novels, plays); it was a sorry extension of pantomime. The only 'author' of a film was the playwright or novelist who had first written the story. In response, Clair enriched the standard definition of the *metteur en scène*—responsible for executing the instructions on the page—by arguing that there was more to directing than following orders. In fact, every *metteur en scène* was actually an *auteur* because he attended to style, costume and performance. Clair's early use of the *auteur* notion versus the *metteur en scène* was weak however, as it drew out only the most superficial aspects of film-making. Pagnol's put-down of 'canned theatre' was closer to the perception shared by even some of the most progressive critics at the time. If there was a creative activity involved in film-making, it came during the process of adapting a work for the screen.

When the Depression eventually reached France in 1934 some of its largest production companies went bankrupt—Gaumont in 1934, Pathé in 1936. The burgeoning independent scene, meanwhile, was hit so hard that even serious critics such as Moussinac decided it was the end: film's avant-garde could never survive in this climate. The search for alternative organization models became an urgent one, in light of the spectacular failure of the big companies and the inevitable decline in domestic film production. In the spring of 1936, the triumphant election of the Popular Front—an alliance of left parties with a common programme of policies and proposed reforms—brought renewed vigour to this search for models other than that derived from the capitalist industry. Education and arts minister Jean Zay proposed a state-controlled umbrella organization to protect the film industry. His idea was eventually realized in 1946 (although Zay himself had been assassinated by Vichy militias at the end of the war) with the foundation of what is still today the state's main cinema institution, the Centre National du Cinéma.

The Popular Front election also encouraged a shift towards more practical action and politically engaged film-making. There had been one particularly progressive development in 1934, with the setting up of the independent organization Ciné-Liberté that built on earlier initiatives, including the abortive Cinéma du Peuple of 1914—intended to redistribute production and distribution for the benefit of the working classes—and Moussinac's Spartacus cine-club of 1927.[5] Led by Jean Renoir, Ciné-Liberté's gained the backing of the Popular Front for its attempt to shift some of the control over cinematic production and creation from the major studios to the working class. Most of its activity went into funding and screening documentaries, many of which were early expressions of *cinéma vérité* and included the collaboration between Hemingway, Dos Passos and Joris Ivens for *Spanish Earth*. However, Ciné-Liberté's lifespan was no longer than that of the Popular Front. An over-budget *La Marseillaise*—Renoir's sympathetic but light history of the storming of the Bastille—sounded its death knell in 1938. Yet, in those four years, Ciné-Liberté instilled the idea in France that such initiatives were at least practically possible.

Leenhardt's little handbook

One of the earliest attempts to address the film critic's particular role and relationship with the public, while promulgating a conception of cinema as an art, was that of critic and film-maker Roger Leenhardt, who wrote a special column for the radical Catholic journal *Esprit* in

---

5 Founders of Le Cinéma du Peuple included anarchist publisher Jean Grave. Its programme is reproduced in Georges Sadoul, *Histoire générale du cinéma*, vol. 3, Paris 1952, p. 272. Léon Moussinac set up Les Amis de Spartacus with his Communist Party colleagues. It was overtly political in orientation, usually exhibiting (banned) Soviet films, but also working to preserve a wide variety of prints. Membership and attendance soared within the first year, rivalling the studio-owned screens and undercutting government censorship. Police disbanded the cine-club in 1928.

1935–6. Looking independently at various elements of film art, his 'little handbook' sought to bring the popular and the artistic together, using the critic as the vital go-between. He explained the challenge:

> You can be moved by a great film without knowing anything special about cinema. But then a specific kind of beauty escapes you. Those . . . who see a film unfold without inwardly sensing 'the shots passing by' only experience the film as the translation of a foreign language. The modest, intimate school for spectators that I would like to initiate has no other pretension than to help those who love the cinema, in some small way, to seize that beauty 'in the text itself'.

The series involved separate articles on topics such as editing, photographic quality, camera angles and movement, and music.[6] The handbook was a milestone: it offered the common viewer in very lucid terms an education on how to see cinema and receive its art. By isolating the technical features that could otherwise pass unnoticed and seeking to communicate the genius at work and true artistry involved, Leenhardt sowed some revolutionary seeds that *Cahiers* writers would bring to full florescence. Leenhardt also made one unprecedented and bold move: he drew his examples exclusively from American, German and Soviet rather than French films.

Occupation and Liberation

The Nazi Occupation of France between 1940 and 1944 had contradictory effects on film culture. Writing became more politicized: on the heels of Popular Front experiments, the war

6 The full series is collected in Roger Leenhardt, *Chroniques de cinéma*, Paris 1986. Maurice Jaubert wrote the last essay, on music. Fellow critic at *Esprit* and composer, Jaubert was responsible for the scores in some of Jean Vigo's films, amongst others, where he had introduced music as 'supplementary poetry' to film. In *Zéro de Conduite* the original score was played backwards as the young boys made their nocturnal procession through the school to stage a revolt against the masters. 'Le Cinéma: La musique', *Esprit* 43, April 1936.

sharpened ideological positions still further. Many had to reorient their priorities, to the frontline, go underground—the journal *Esprit* lasted six issues in the Free Zone before editor Emmanuel Mounier was imprisoned—or leave the country altogether. Actor Jean Gabin and director Julien Duvivier were among the most high-profile figures in the film industry to head to America. And yet, paradoxically, wartime was a good period for French cinema. The public was so hungry for escapism that 280 screens from a possible 310 reopened in Paris in 1940, having been shut down when the Germans initially occupied the city; attendance rose from 220 million in 1938 to 304 million in 1943. Output was respectable too, despite difficult conditions and Vichy censorship. In this period Marcel Carné, Renoir and Henri-Georges Clouzot produced some important works, with *Les Enfants du paradis*, *La Grande illusion* and *Le Corbeau*.

France was filled with a mixture of elation and economic hardship after the war. The fresh experience of camaraderie amongst resisters was tempered by a newly felt moral uncertainty, brought on by the purges of collaborators that now rocked intellectual and artistic circles. Clouzot was forced into exile after it was revealed that *Le Corbeau* had been produced by Continental, a German-run company before it was nationalized in 1944. Economically, the situation was dire: a million and a half French citizens were still in Germany, as prisoners of war, deportees or conscripted workers; the country's infrastructure had been devastated, badly hampering the distribution of food and other essentials. Recovery would be slow with France's economic base ravaged by Allied bombings, sabotage, and Germany's drain on its machinery and labour. By 1947 the situation remained difficult: bread rationing was reintroduced, and between September and May the next year low salaries and high prices provoked waves of strikes and demonstrations. The political future was also uncertain: the Fourth Republic limped on, under pressure as much from De Gaulle as the Communist Party. Both had emerged from the war with heroic credentials—De Gaulle as the face of Free France, the PCF as the *parti des 75 000 fusillés*—and both vied for support in forthcoming elections.

Cinematic culture thrived as soon as it was freed from the semiclandestinity imposed by the Occupation. The audience was bigger than ever and the national industry had remained consistent, if restricted. A network of left-wing cine-clubs was set up in Paris, many under the control of the PCF, which looked to culture as a key recruiting ground. Georges Sadoul, Party member and resident critic at *Les Lettres françaises*, was its spokesman. Extremely partisan, he nevertheless retained respect from most quarters for being one film's first serious historians.

Guardian of treasures

Another figure of paramount importance in these years was Henri Langlois. In 1935 he had set up with his friend Georges Franju the Cercle du Cinéma cine-club. Langlois' approach to programming was unique—'there is a whole science of camouflage behind a good programme, it is like what we called *haute couture*. The stitching is invisible; links are made between the films; things happen, something similar to when paintings are hung in an exhibition: wonderful surprises are possible'.[7] A year later he founded the Cinémathèque Française, conceived as a private, autonomous repository of national and film-related heritage. Langlois was instrumental during the war in keeping Parisian film culture alive and vibrant. He put on many underground screenings for friends (Simone Signoret would first see *Battleship Potemkin* in 1941, in Langlois's mother's dining room) and also worked tirelessly with Germaine Dulac, a key go-between with the Germans, to save films under threat of seizure and destruction.[8]

The Cinémathèque actually emerged stronger after the war. In 1944 it secured state subsidies, and with the international pedigree

7 *Le Monde*, 15 January 1977.

8 The fear of material loss had haunted Langlois from childhood. In 1922, aged eight, he had been forced to flee his home town of Izmir, following the Turkish assault on the Greek population that resulted in four-fifths of the city burning down. His family lost everything in the fires. Edgardo Cozarinsky's 1994 biographical film, *Citizen Langlois*, begins with a suitcase bursting into flames. For a history of the Cinémathèque and part-biography of Langlois, see Laurent Mannoni, *Histoire de la Cinémathèque Française*, Paris 2006.

gained after the archival wartime activity of Langlois it quickly extended its network around the world. Many associated 'Amis de la Cinémathèque Française' were set up in Algeria, Morocco and Tunisia. Langlois took advantage of the post-war influx of Hollywood cinema, following the release of a five-year backlog of films after their suspended distribution during the war: screenings of silent classics alternated with (unsubtitled) Hawks, Hitchcock and *film noir* in the rue de Messine. These programmes played a major role in nurturing cinephile tastes, as well as shaping research in film history.

Early battle cries

Among a spate of new film journals, *L'Ecran Français* had Sartre, Camus, Malraux, Jacques Becker and Langlois on its editorial board. It published foundational texts that would be incipient formulations of the allegiance to particular directors in opposition to others—the *politique des auteurs*—such as Alexandre Astruc's piece on the *caméra-stylo* (camera-pen), which invoked a notion of the film director as an individual artist comparable to a painter or an author, wielding his production unit as a novelist his fountain pen; while Leenhardt continued in the internationalist spirit of his pre-war handbook to call for spectators and critics to choose between Ford and Wyler.[9] Maurice Scherer (soon to take the pseudonym Eric Rohmer, from Erich von Stroheim and Sax Rohmer, creator of Fu Manchu) was editing *Gazette du cinéma*, the bulletin of the Quartier Latin cine-club.[10] In 1946, the *bon-viveur* cinephile Jean-Georges Auriol relaunched his pre-war *Revue du cinéma*, with a mission to challenge the golden-ageism that idealized the silent era and combat the nationalist praise heaped on the *cinéma de qualité* of Marcel Carné and René Clair. Convinced that criticism of cinema required a particular language of its own, Auriol looked to the avant-garde, to Italy, and to the work of Welles, Sturges and Wyler in

9 Alexandre Astruc, 'Naissance d'une nouvelle avant-garde: la caméra-stylo'; Roger Leenhardt, 'A bas Ford, vive Wyler', *L'Ecran Français*, 30 March and 13 April 1948.

10 The magazine, which focused especially on Hollywood westerns, *noirs* and melodramas, appeared for only two issues in 1949.

the US. In the glossy, prestigious magazine published by Gallimard—to the disapproval of Camus, in a neighbouring office, who felt it was a waste of resources—Auriol published a mixture of established and younger critics, bringing together Jacques Doniol-Valcroze (working at *Cinémonde*), Astruc, Pierre Kast, Bazin and Rohmer; Auriol's own essays on cinema and painting remain seminal texts.

The last modernist project

By 1950, the post-Liberation ebullience had begun to ebb as Cold War pressures set in. The PCF extended a more rigid control over *L'Ecran Français* and some of the cine-clubs. Divisions widened. Georges Sadoul represented the old-guard consensus: the silent era was to be treated with reverence, Hollywood with disdain, and national products with uncritical enthusiasm. By contrast, the group gathering around what was soon to become the *Cahiers* project was united not only by its passionate cinephilia but by its insistence on the need for a rupture with established cinematographic practice and theory. For them, as Peter Wollen has put it, 'the complete overthrow of the existing regime of taste was a precondition for the triumph of new film-makers with new films, demanding to be judged on a different scale of values.' This paradigm shift was 'the last of a series of twentieth-century critical revolutions in the name of "modernism"', against an *ancien régime* of artistic convention.[11] In this struggle, the New World was seen as a cultural ally, a potent image-maker of modernity and the dynamic popular energies within it. The name *Cahiers*—suggesting notes scribbled in school exercise books—indicates the preliminary, if deeply serious, nature of the enterprise.

America had been a cultural attractor in the years before and immediately after the war. The styles of Hemingway, Faulkner or Dos Passos were inspiring the students of Balzac and Baudelaire, arriving, as Malraux put it, 'like eruptions of Greek tragedy in the detective story'. Two-thirds of the manuscripts Sartre had to read for *Les Temps modernes*

11 Peter Wollen, *Paris Hollywood: Writings on Film*, London 2002, p. 218.

were written *à la* Hemingway. When Sartre tried to convey the reasons for his own high praise, he explained that their often harsh portrayals of American society 'never put us off America—on the contrary, we saw in it a manifestation of [the country's] liberty'. The iniquities of racism or poverty explored in these novels resonated with experiences in France, Sartre said. They were a sign of the 'imperfections of our time', and American writers had developed a technique that enabled the reader to intuitively grasp the acts and motivations of characters, 'because he sees them being born and formed in a situation which has been made intelligible to him. They live because they spurt suddenly from a deep well. To analyse them would be to kill them.'[12]

The constellation forming at *Cahiers* was an exceptionally heterogeneous one in its range of tastes and approaches. Bazin was influenced by the anti-colonial Catholicism of Emmanuel Mounier at *Esprit*, as well as by Sartre; Rohmer was a high formalist Joseph-Marie Lo Duca, a well-known, 'chic' critic and author of *Histoire du cinéma* in the *Que sais-je?* series had good connections in Parisian publishing; Doniol-Valcroze has an admirer of Buñuel. Kast was the only committed leftist of the group. The final ingredient would come from the polemical dynamism of a still younger group: Truffaut (Bazin's protégé), Godard, Rivette, Chabrol. These 'young Turks' congregated at cine-club screenings, and some wrote for Scherer/Rohmer's *Gazette*. Bazin acted as an important liaison at first, bringing into the youthful iconoclasts the more established and influential Parisian critical circles. It was at the 'Festival du Film Maudit' in Biarritz in 1949, organized by Bazin, Cocteau, Bresson and Raymond Queneau, that the young Turks emerged as a concerted force. There the twenty-year-olds rehearsed in heated conversations positions they would soon immortalize in print.[13] The final catalyst came with the sudden death of Auriol in a car crash

12 Jean-Paul Sartre, 'American Novelists in French Eyes', *Atlantic Monthly*, August 1946.

13 This festival, named by Cocteau after Verlaine's phrase describing Rimbaud, Mallarmé and others as 'les poètes maudits', had the aim of celebrating, with all the pomp of Cannes, the films the cinema establishment had sought to condemn. Bresson, Ford, Tati, Vigo and Welles all appeared on the festival programme in 1949.

in 1950. This tragedy brought the *Revue* to an end, the only publication at least partly satisfying the young critics' idea of what a film magazine should be. A year later, issue number one of *Cahiers* arrived on the newsstands. For the first time the 'jotter' devoted to cinema gathered its pages and detonated the pent-up contents into fifties Parisian cinephile culture, and beyond.

Samuel Fuller, *I Shot Jesse James* (1949)

2

1951–1959
The Yellow Years

The elegant thirty-page magazine that appeared each month signalled, with a large black-and-white photograph on its mustard-yellow cover, the most admired film of the moment. The use of the still, without recourse to any headlines, conveyed the absolute primacy that *Cahiers du cinéma* would give to the engagement with the aesthetics of cinema. The 'yellow *Cahiers*', as the journal has been called retrospectively,[1] contained four or five articles in total. Bound in its pages, just under A4 in size, were reviews plus a few longer pieces that looked closely at a director's work, or explored film technique; sometimes a 'letter' came from a festival or another country, or an in-depth interview was conducted with one revered master. Arresting photographs interspersed the texts and might take up a whole page as equal value was given to the writing on film and its captured memory. All these elements combined to produce an aesthetic masterpiece: through its simple, bold layout and composition alone, *Cahiers*, just as an object, paid homage to the

1 The name for the early *Cahiers* format, invoked to distinguish it from its later incarnations, was originally the title of another arts journal from the 1930s with which it should not be confused. *Les Cahiers jaunes* has a very different background: it emerged out of a coalition of Surrealists, Marxists and former members of Le Grand Jeu, a group of metaphysical writers who rivalled the Surrealists in the late twenties and early thirties.

beauty of cinema. Financial backing came from Léonide Kiegel and his publishing house, Editions de l'Etoile; initial readership was inherited from the small number of subscribers to the now closed *Revue du cinéma*.

Lessons from André Bazin

In its first decade, the two critics who successively led the editorial team were from the older generation: André Bazin (b. 1918) and Eric Rohmer (b. 1920). Both men were Catholics, both had trained as schoolteachers and then turned to film criticism; in other respects they were quite different in formation and approach. In the 1950s, Bazin's influence was pedagogic and paternal, rather than polemical. When *Cahiers* was founded he was thirty-three, with a strong international reputation as a film critic under his belt. Prior to this he had attended the Ecole Normale Supérieure at Saint-Cloud, where he took part in a number of reading groups that involved exploring important ideas of the period, in particular Henri Bergson's theories of perception. It was at one such group organized by *Esprit* that he first met this journal's editor, Emmanuel Mounier, whose socially radical Catholicism stayed with Bazin throughout his life. As well as its theological positions, Bazin was drawn to its social conscience and dedication to cultural enlightenment and liberation.

In the pages of *Esprit* Bazin also came across the extraordinary film criticism of Roger Leenhardt, particularly his series written in the Popular Front years. Bazin was struck by Leenhardt's proposition that cinema's primary value was attained through its adaptation to things as they are. Rendering was more valuable than signifying through metaphors in the narrative structure. For Leenhardt, cinema was an 'always partial view of something significant that tries to appear through it'. A director was thus more a student than a teacher of the universe. Bazin found in this a compelling framework through which to develop his own ontology of cinema. It seemed that the medium offered an unprecedented access to reality, allowing the viewer to see the deeper—religious—beauty, which ordinarily escaped the naked eye.[2]

The second influence on Bazin regarding ideas on cinema was André Malraux. Through his 'Sketch for a Psychology of the Cinema' (1940) and *Museum Without Walls*, published in 1947, Malraux inspired Bazin to do for cinema what he had sought to achieve with the traditional arts: imbue it with a sense of destiny, trace back its origins to deep human psychological necessities and illustrate how successive styles are the product of an evolving social function. For Malraux, and for Bazin, art should be understood as the developing expression of the human spirit, in response to the changing forms of the human condition.

Bazin's institutional career foundered when he was refused a teaching post because of his stammer. During the war he was stationed in Pau, after failing the military test to join the front line. Bazin engaged in resistance activities, first by setting up the magazine *Recontres* and then in 1941 by joining the cultural organization Maison des Lettres, where he worked with students displaced by the fighting and ran underground screenings in defiance of Nazi authorities.

Earthly magic of the camera

After the Liberation Bazin intensified his writing activity and devoted himself almost entirely to cinema. He joined the editorial board of *Esprit* and also worked with *Les Temps modernes*, where he exchanged ideas with another key influence on his developing theory of cinema: Sartre. Bazin had already been schooled in Bergsonianism during the thirties and forties, and was taken with Sartre's incorporation of phenomenology in his own idea of the *image-pensée*: 'the image is a certain type of consciousness, an act and not a thing . . . it is the

2 Leenhardt is the film critic most often cited as the major influence on Bazin. However, the work of Jean Epstein must also be mentioned, notably his idea of cinema 'creating a new system of "lyrosophical" cognition that could reveal the unconscious mysteries of nature, and human nature, through epistemological exploration of time as well as space.' Richard Abel links Bazin, Epstein and Sartre in their conceptions of nature. Abel, *French Film Theory and Criticism*, pp. 14–15, 156–7, 176, n. 89.

consciousness of some thing'.[3] Bazin was especially fascinated by the nature of the moving image, believing that the power of the camera lay 'not in what it adds to reality but in what it reveals of it'—a recorder of the world that made manifest the providence of creation.[4] He perceived this realism in the works of Renoir, his favourite director; Rossellini; and, as he argued in a *Temps modernes* debate with Sartre, Welles.[5]

Bazin combined the phenomenological approach with a deeply rooted spirituality. Whilst he rejected any organized form of religion, a constant theological strain is discernible in his work. For Claude Bellanger, founding editor of *Le Parisien libéré*, Bazin was 'the missionary of a young art to which he consecrated his immense moral force'.[6] Evolutionary theorist Pierre Teilhard de Chardin proposed a teleological understanding of the world that strengthened Bazin's conviction that there were latent truths in nature, an internal consciousness striving to be liberated.[7] Thus Bazin watched films with the same fascination as he felt observing the many animals he kept at home, captivated by the mixture of strict order and spontaneity, restraint and freedom that determined both. 'His way of loving cinema was a way of loving through cinema, just as he loved parrots, chameleons, serpents, all the creatures of the natural world, and men too.'[8] Bazin's writing conveyed this sense of revelation he experienced before cinema: films taught him about both life and art and he wrote

---

3 Jean-Paul Sartre, *L'Imagination* [1936], Paris 2003, p. 162.

4 André Bazin, *Qu'est-ce que le cinéma?*, vol. 1 [1958], Paris 2002, p. 67.

5 For Sartre's critique of Welles's storytelling in *Citizen Kane*, see 'Quand Hollywood veut faire penser . . .', *L'Ecran Français*, August 1945. In defence, Bazin argued that no judgement on the film should rest solely on its success as linear narrative: 'La technique de *Citizen Kane*' was published in *Les Temps modernes*, no. 17, 1947. Both are collected in Roger Leenhardt, *Chroniques de cinéma*, Paris 1978.

6 Bellanger, speaking at Bazin's funeral in 1958, quoted in Dudley Andrew's indispensible biography, *André Bazin*, Oxford 1978, p. 2.

7 A member of the Jesuit order, Teilhard had been exiled to China and his work was censored by the Church. In the forties and fifties it enjoyed a small revival in France.

8 Alexandre Astruc, *Cahiers* 91, January 1959.

with the verve of an excited student, who, having just understood something, wants at once to share this new knowledge.

Bazin's first article on cinema appeared in 1944 in *Le Parisien libéré*. The paper had been published underground during the resistance and went on to become France's largest morning paper. Bazin contributed well over 600 pieces to it, including early articles whetting readers' appetites for the forthcoming windfall of American films once the embargo was lifted, and the 'Little School of the Spectator', a series started in 1946 in homage to Leenhardt's pioneering *Esprit* series over a decade earlier.[9] After the war Bazin joined the newly founded culture organization Travail et Culture, which aspired to bring culture into factories and industrial organizations. He also began to set up cine-clubs around the country. By 1947 he had expanded the ventures to other parts of Europe and North Africa. Bazin travelled everywhere, and his film introductions and post-screening discussions inspired many who attended the sessions. On one trip to Germany, the event proved so popular that half the audience was forced to watch the film from behind the projection screen. Despite the circumstances, according to one member of the audience, Bazin's message was transmitted with such clarity and passion that 'it has not since stopped stirring tempests in the German conception of cinema'.[10]

Transmission and Tarzan

Bazin's criticism was profoundly social, in both practice and aspiration. In this sense he was reaffirming the historical link between the popular and the experimental avant-garde that had marked the spirit of the twenties. Bazin brought to this his own Catholic social radicalism, and believed that as a critic he could encourage a change in the audience's notion of itself—helping viewers to develop from passive consumers into co-creators. If an audience laid claim to their cinema, they could learn to take command of their whole culture.

9 Bazin's enormous output is being collected in the *Tout Bazin* project, led by André Labarthe.

10 Quoted in Andrew, *André Bazin*, p. 95.

Bazin's cine-club programmes were driven by this aspiration to make the audience look first at the film, and then at its function, but in such a way that engaged with the shared memory of the film. As Claude Roy would recall, Bazin 'showed you the movie you should have seen and made you feel as if you had in fact seen it'.[11]

The biggest public controversy in Bazin's career came in 1950, in the increasingly polarized atmosphere of the Cold War. Bazin always avoided directly political readings of film, and in an article for *Esprit*, 'The myth of Stalin and Soviet cinema' he drew a parallel between the Russian leader and Tarzan. When introduced in a film, both had the effect of reducing every aspect of the story to the destiny of one figure. Tarzan, Bazin concluded, was preferable because at least his films were subject to popular scrutiny at the box office, whereas Russian cinema received full distribution regardless of the public verdict. For Sadoul and the Communist Party, such an opinion was tantamount to choosing Hollywood studios over the socialist concept of art promoted by the Soviet system. After this, Bazin's association with Travail et Culture was over.

In 1951, then, Bazin was highly respected and his reputation well established; it was also controversial. *Cahiers* would be the final flourish. In reality Bazin was comparatively more detached towards this journal than towards previous projects, largely as a result of his ailing health. His generational separation from the youngest critics meant he stepped frequently into the role of the diplomat—he was experienced enough to realize that if the journal were to survive it could not afford to burn its bridges too quickly with every influential film critic in Paris. Theoretically too, Bazin provided the foundations on which the young team could build their subsequent ideas. His evolutionary outlook allowed, for example, the hagiography of the great directors *Cahiers* inaugurated, validating the old masters as well as hitherto neglected practitioners such as Robert Flaherty and Jean Vigo. In the final years of his life, Bazin was increasingly forced to retreat to his home in the countryside, and often bed-bound. As a result he wrote a number of articles about television, welcoming the

11 Claude Roy, *Cahiers* 91, January 1959.

mix of realism and imagination in the new TV dramas shot in real time; precursors to the faster filming schedules of the New Wave. Although Bazin ceded editorial control to the young Turks as early as 1954, he had established *Cahiers*' intellectual bedrock. During his lifetime he left a mark in nearly every copy of *Cahiers*—74 out of 90 issues ran articles by Bazin—and the relevance of his ideas is still explored in its page today.

New axiomatic programme

The spirit of the young Turks was passionate and polemical, and by 1954 it was their *va-t'en guerre* approach that dominated *Cahiers*' manifestos. One of the most controversial positions was 'Hitchcocko–Hawksianism'—the passionate defence of both film-makers as masters of the art. This was the *politique des auteurs* in embryonic form. Another catalyst that brought the young Turks together in opposition was old-guard scepticism and conservatism. Pierre Kast, a contemporary of the group, but a frequent critic for *L'Ecran*, more sympathetic to Sadoul's outlook, saw a so-called 'Scherer School' emerging after Godard's praise for *Strangers on a Train* in 1952. As a retort, Rohmer (still writing as Maurice Scherer) published 'On Three Films and a Particular School', in which he elevated Hitchcock to the pantheon of great directors, and named *I Confess* a modern masterpiece. Delighted to take on the role Kast had attributed to him, Rohmer set out the aims of the new 'school': 'My wish for film criticism is that it free itself at last from the ideas dictated to it by its elders, and be able to consider, with fresh eyes and mind, the works that, in my opinion, count far more in the history of our age than the pale survivors of an art that is no more.'[12] In the same issue Jacques Rivette outlined the genius of Howard Hawks.

The new critical tone was definitively set in January 1954, with François Truffaut's polemic, 'A Certain Tendency in French Cinema'. That essay marked the birth of the real spirit of *Cahiers*, Doniol-Valcroze later concluded. In a style that was aggressive,

12 *Cahiers* 26, August–September 1953.

urgent and personal, Truffaut attacked traditional cinema in favour of selected *auteurs*. He accused the former, with its penchant for literary adaptations, of negating the specificity of cinema by applying an 'equivalence principle' between book and film: the ensuing work was the antithesis of realism. Photographs of each guilty screenwriter or director—Jean Aurenche, Clouzot and Jean Delannoy among them—were printed alongside the text like mug shots, adding to the sense of exposure. It was a spirited outburst, perhaps even boorish, Truffaut admitted; but it was either that or cowardice, and it was time critics dispensed with drawing-room niceties.

Up to this point Bazin and Doniol-Valcroze had tempered the young Turks' excesses by diplomatically publishing counter-views, such as Bazin's own criticisms of Hitchcock, or the travel essays by Sadoul. But with 'A Certain Tendency', the *politique des auteurs* had been formulated into an axiomatic programme. Unlike a mere director, an *auteur* was a film-maker with a vision of the world enunciated through his *mise en scène*: it was not the particular subject but the way the author chose to treat it that was important; in the hands of a master, the flimsiest detective story could become a great work. Viewing therefore involved not a concentration on the content but on this cinematic staging, which was where the *auteur*'s 'griffe', or mark, could be grasped. Even—perhaps especially—the worst films of an *auteur* were to be appreciated in this fashion, in contrast to an œuvre-by-œeuvre analysis. In Doniol-Valcroze's words again: with Truffaut's article 'something bound us together. From then on it was known that we were for Renoir, Rossellini, Hitchcock . . . and against X, Y and Z.'[13] Each critic had their personal favourites—for Rivette it was Hawks, for Truffaut, Hitchcock, for Godard, Nicholas Ray—and in the spirit of the *politique*, each new film would be reviewed by the one who was most enthusiastic about it. The aim was, after all, to convince readers that these men were masters of the art. Subsequent contents reflected the canon-building nature of this approach: major interviews explored in detail a particular director's

13 *Cahiers* 100, October 1959.

work; the first with Jacques Becker was held in 1954.[14] A 'Council of Ten' ratings list appeared from 1955, with each new release graded from blob ('don't bother'), one star ('to be seen at a pinch'), two stars ('to be seen'), three stars ('must be seen') to four stars ('masterpiece'). An annual list of best directors and films was inaugurated that year. Initially, Ingmar Bergman, Bresson, Mizoguchi, Ray and Rossellini topped most critics' nominations. Yet in an association of such strong personalities, powerful differences persisted. Rohmer always affirmed his commitment to the combination of *politique des auteurs* and *mise en scène*, which he understood as the art of cinema;[15] but in a 'family quarrel' in 1957 Bazin was already chiding his young colleagues about the shortcomings of this approach, provoked by Jean Domarchi's glowing review of Vincente Minnelli's pap Technicolor biopic of Van Gogh, *Lust for Life*. As an art, Bazin argued, cinema was also both popular and industrial, and these factors meant a more nuanced account was needed. More broadly, any artist had their good or bad days: 'Voltaire was a horrible playwright when he thought he was Racine's successor and a storyteller of genius when he made the parable a vehicle for the ideas that would shatter the eighteenth century.' Of the equation, 'author + subject = work', the *politique* perspective retained only the author. Bazin warned against the dangers of instituting 'an aesthetic personality cult'.[16]

Eclecticism of the young Turks

Each writer brought his own critical tools and concepts for viewing film. Rivette, 'the soul of the group', was unique in his grasp of *mise*

---

14 In the same year Renoir, Buñuel and Rossellini met the young editors. Chabrol and Truffaut then came up against Hitchcock. The anticipated encounter proved disappointing. The director was unforthcoming, playing on misunderstandings (good or God, evil or Devil). His interviewers consoled each other with the thought that if, conscious of his genius, Hitchcock was the greatest liar ever, and that made him the most Hitchcockian character of all.

15 Rohmer in interview, *Cahiers* 172, November 1965.

16 *Cahiers* 70, April 1957.

en scène, this 'architecture of relations, moving and yet suspended in space . . . [like a] diamond: transparent yet with ambiguous reflections, sharp and cutting edges' that allowed critics to see beyond the constraints of studio demands, scenarios and budgets to distinguish an *auteur* from the rest.[17] Godard's early contributions were vintage *politique des auteurs*. He showed a taste for the strange and paradoxical, and was particularly adept at analysing the 'minor' films of a director, their 'revealing failures'. It was Godard who first reviewed Bergman's work in the journal in 1958, while he could also write in praise of minor westerns:

> The Americans, who are much more stupid when it comes to analysis, instinctively bring off very complex scripts. They also have a gift for the kind of simplicity which bestows depth—in a little western like *Ride the High Country*, for instance. If one tries to do something like that in France, one looks like an intellectual. The Americans are real and natural, but this attitude has a meaning over there. We in France must find something that has a meaning—find the French attitude as they have found the American attitude. To do so, one must begin by talking about things one knows.[18]

Early contributions on Nicholas Ray bring out the distinctiveness of each critic. Rivette addressed his readers with a set of elegant imperatives: this must be loved, that must be recognized—a style of criticism always conscious of the spectator he had to convince. For Godard, with characteristically infectious grandeur, '*Bitter Victory*, like the sun, makes you close your eyes. Truth is blinding.'[19] Truffaut was aggressive, prescriptive and darkly comical:

> Those who [have not seen Ray's films] will just have to trust me, and that will be their little punishment . . . You can refute Hawks in the

17 *Cahiers* 32, February 1954.
18 Godard in interview, *Cahiers* 138, December 1962.
19 *Cahiers* 79, January 1958.

> name of Ray, but to anyone who would reject them both, I would just say this: stop going to the cinema, don't watch any more films, for you will never know the meaning of . . . a frame, a shot, an idea, a good film, the cinema.[20]

Rohmer was always more sober, though no less enraptured. 'May I be forgiven my favourite vice', he asked readers, 'of evoking the memory of the ancient Greeks' to read *Rebel Without a Cause* as a 'drama in five acts'.[21] The contrast was instructive: Godard and Rivette celebrated the unprecedented in Ray; Rohmer drew out timeless issues of morality and tragedy.

Cinephile orphans

For its young critics, *Cahiers* was like a surrogate family. Fathers, godfathers, adoptive sons—it is a story, as Serge Daney has described it, 'of stubborn orphans and chosen families', the young spectators weaving their own histories with those they saw on screen.[22] Truffaut, for example, born in 1932 to a 'father unknown' and brought up initially in a foster home and then by his grandmother, was arrested at the age of fifteen for running a cine-club on stolen funds. Bazin, having met the boy at the opening night of his illegal venture, intervened to rescue him from the juvenile detention centre and virtually adopted him. He would secure Truffaut's release from prison again in 1951, when the teenager went AWOL from the army on the eve of embarkation for Indo-China.

Out of necessity or otherwise—parents lost in the war, an early departure from home, or simply missed classes at university—cinema replaced the family or academic studies. Both Rivette and Godard

20 Written under the pseudonym Robert Lachenay, *Cahiers* 46, April 1955.

21 *Cahiers* 59, May 1956.

22 Serge Daney, *Devant la recrudescence des vols de sacs à main*, Lyon 1997, p. 97. Daney had in mind, as a model of the film-struck orphan, the young John Mohune in Fritz Lang's *Moonfleet* who designated chief smuggler Jeremy Fox as his friend, took his hand and would not let go. The act distilled the passionate faith of the cinephile who has chosen cinema as his guide.

arrived in Paris to study at the Sorbonne, but gravitated instead to the Cinémathèque and film journals, and found their education there. Cinephile culture had its own forms of erudition, its lectures, pupils and teachers: 'in the cine-clubs [we found] our night classes . . . our books . . . wary of intellectuals, universities and politics, protected from all exterior intervention'.[23] Truffaut, who had seen *The Rules of the Game* at least twenty times, kept meticulous files on every film; close, repeated watching was intrinsic to his criticism. He was unequivocal: 'Let us not respect, not follow, not read, not be interested by and not like anyone but the specialists.'[24]

Aesthetics and politics

The history of *Cahiers* inevitably involves blind spots as well as spotlights. In its first decade other artistic movements were considered unimportant, with theatre and the *nouveau roman* ignored, although Brecht was an influential early discovery in 1960. Cinemas of the Third World and newer avant-garde work entered the journal with some delay. The revolutionary Soviet films of the twenties were mostly snubbed as part of a broader resistance to Sadoul's 'Stalinist criticism'—Boris Barnet was chosen over Eisenstein by Rivette in 1953—and it was not until the seventies that the Russian line was seriously reconsidered.[25] The exclusive choice of *auteurs* left some genres, especially fantasy and animation films, largely unexplored, with the exception of texts by critics André Martin and Fereydoun Hoveyda. The anarchic surrealism of Buñuel baffled the more classical tastes. A larger absence was that of politics. *Cahiers* virtually ignored both Indo-China and the Algerian

---

23 *Cahiers* 45, March 1955. Also see Truffaut's article, 'Les sept péchés capitaux de la critique', *Arts*, April 1955.

24 Baecque, *La Cinéphilie*, p. 20.

25 There would be a thawing of relations in the sixties when Sadoul—who never addressed the Khrushchev report publicly, but gradually effaced Stalin from his historical narrative—turned his attention to films being made around the world, finding solace for his disappointed militancy in international and youth cinema. He would embrace the New Wave, as well as works by Rocha, Pasolini and Bertolucci.

war. Godard summed up the journal's attitude at the time: 'I have moral and psychological intentions which are defined through situations born of political events. That's all.'[26]

This inevitably drew accusations of conservativism and right-wing criticism, as the young critics seemed more concerned with paying homage to Hollywood and gushing about B-movies than with addressing any of the political concerns of the moment, or finding their trace in cinema. *Cahiers*' initial rejection of politics can be understood as a logical extension of the project to elevate film and criticism to the level of indisputable art, through evocation of the conscious genius at work behind the images. *Seeing* film therefore meant addressing first and foremost the *mise en scène* as a distinctive tableau put in place by the director, which in turn presented a coherent and unique world view. No ideological reading or political sympathy was necessary prior to this, and imposing it would inevitably produce a biased 'reading' of the film that failed to *look* at its visual composition.[27] The *Cahiers* line went against the general critical climate. Bazin's Tarzan experience was an early sign that the Cold War was putting critics under increasing pressure to choose their camp and practise politics through their film writing. In 1953 distributors followed Sadoul's characterization of Fuller's *Pickup on South Street*, modifying its title (to *Port of Drugs*) and storyline—the pickpocket intercepts a drug shipment, rather than the microfilm destined for the communists—before releasing it in France.[28] For the young Turks, politics did

26 Interview in *Cahiers* 138, December 1962.

27 Contributions from two 'Hollywoodophile communists', Louis Marcolles and Jean Domarchi, were exceptions. Marcolles defended the possibility of being a discerning critic of Soviet cinema and passionate defender of John Ford whilst at the same time remaining Marxist; Domarchi, economist and writer at *Les Temps modernes*, was a specialist in the cinemas of Minnelli, Hitchcock and Mann. In October 1956 his strongly anti-Stalinist text offered a Marxist reading of the genius of Hollywood cinematography. Also see Antoine de Baecque, *Histoire d'une revue. 1. A l'assaut du cinéma, 1951–1959*, Paris 1991, pp. 210–13. Henceforth references to the two volumes will be 'Baecque I' and 'Baecque II'.

28 Samuel Fuller, *A Third Face: My Tale of Writing, Fighting and Filmmaking*, New York 2002, pp. 304–6.

nothing but confuse one's engagement with cinema. They explicitly rejected its method, which they saw as developing pre-determined arguments with only instrumental reference to film. Critics on this path failed at the level of cinematic judgement.

The conscious apoliticism at *Cahiers* was in strong contrast to the explicitly anti-colonial film journal *Positif*. Founded in 1952 and initially associated with the PCF, it quickly developed a strong surrealist influence.[29] In the words of its editor, Robert Benayoun, *Positif* was 'very anti-aesthetic . . . We wanted cinema to express ideas that change society; we wanted it to be an engaged art form.'[30] Compared to the contents of *Cahiers*, *Positif* ran much less on Hollywood and more on Latin America and the Third World; it was less fixated with *auteurs* and gave more attention to genres; it was open to surrealist work and experimental film-makers including Chris Marker, Alain Resnais and Agnès Varda. Whilst Rivette praised the spiritual turn in Rossellini's *Voyage to Italy*, *Positif*'s verdict was that it was a sell-out: the film marked the decline of neo-realism's unflinching, honest portrayal of Resistance and post-war hardship, retreating instead into domestic fable. In fact, Rivette's defence of the film was the clearest expression of the personal register used by *Cahiers* critics. Rivette's 'Letter to Rossellini' also marked the apogee of the *mise en scène* as the dominant object of study at the magazine, attaining here a metaphysical quality. For Rivette, Rossellini's frame was all-

---

29 Ado Kyrou and Robert Benayoun joined *Positif* from the surrealist *L'Age du cinéma*; Eric Losfeld, director of the erotico-surrealist publishing house, Le Terrain Vague, arrived in 1959.

30 Robert Benayoun, cited in Baecque, *La Cinéphilie*, p. 231. *Positif* was closely involved in the Algerian struggle for independence, providing funds to the FLN and signing the September 1960 'Manifesto 121', the declaration of the right to refuse military service in the war. No *Cahiers* editor appeared on the original list, but Doniol-Valcroze, Truffaut and Kast signed a complementary one shortly afterwards. The Manifesto was not published in any French newspaper, though it was mentioned briefly in *Le Monde*. The October issue of *Les Temps modernes* had two blank pages in the place where the Manifesto was due to appear after it was refused at the last stage by the printers. David Drake, *Intellectuals and Politics in Post-War France*, Basingstoke 2002, pp. 123 and 228, n. 83.

consuming; his secret as a director was to move with 'unremitting freedom, and one single, simple motion, through manifest eternity: the world of the incarnation . . . thereafter we too can barely leave this inner circle any more, this basic refrain that is reprised chorally: that the body is the soul, the other is myself, the object is the truth and the message; and now we are also trapped by this place where the passage from one shot to the next is perpetual and infinitely reciprocal; where Matisse's arabesques are not just invisibly linked to their hearth, do not merely represent it, but are the fire itself'. Rivette judged Rossellini's film to be a triumph according to strictly formalist and philosophical–theological standards.[31]

Overall, *Positif* and *Cahiers* oscillated between amicable relations—sharing contributors (Hoveyda, Kast) and common interests—and an outright *guerre de papier*. Rohmer considered the team 'a sect who judge cinema using criteria totally alien to the seventh art',[32] whilst those at *Positif* cast their counterparts in a disparaging light as censors, metaphysical critics, imperialists, mystics or fascists. But as the decade came to an end, *Cahiers* was thriving: strong ideas, foundational concepts, enemies on whom to focus critical energies, admired masters to defend. A major shift was about to take place, however: the journal had been a genuine *stylo-caméra*, to paraphrase Alexandre Astruc, but the young Turks were now ready to pick up the *caméra-stylo*. Many of *Cahiers*' first generation of critics moved into film-making. The New Wave they created ensured the magazine's place in history, but the upswell also led to the first major editorial crisis in the offices on the Champs-Elysées.

31 *Cahiers* 46, April 1955.
32 Baecque I, p. 143.

Jean-Luc Godard, *Vivre sa vie* (1963)

3

1959–1966
Marble to Modern Chemistry

Between 1959 and 1963, the masterworks of the New Wave—Truffaut's *The 400 Blows*, *Shoot the Pianist*, *Jules and Jim*; Godard's *Breathless*, *A Woman is a Woman*, *It's My Life*; Rivette's *Paris Belongs to Us*; Chabrol's *The Cousins*—were made with light mobile cameras and on shoestring budgets. They combined dazzling formal innovation in the framing of shots and the use of sound with a striking ethnography of contemporary France, while enacting the *Cahiers* dictum that 'the only true criticism of a film is another film'.[33] The very radicalism of these works demanded a new agenda at *Cahiers*, but the immediate impact of the New Wave proved double-edged and led to a paradoxical situation at the journal: triumph and turmoil.

Young French directors were dispensing with old rules at the same time as the previously celebrated American cinema was beginning to lose its charm and quality. The old masters were turning out their last, sometimes disappointing works. Domestically, politics was encroaching on the public conscience as the relative silence over one old French colony—Vietnam—was replaced by heated resistance to or defence of nascent Algerian independence. The war in North Africa dominated news and intellectual debates: Henri Alleg's book *La Question*, published in 1958, had exposed the French army's use of torture; Sartre, Camus and Aron split

33 Rivette, *Cahiers* 84, June 1958.

over their contrasting positions, as Sartre pledged solidarity with the liberation struggle, Camus's *pied-noir* background complicated and eventually depoliticized his stance, and Aron supported the continuation of French Algeria.

The detached cinephilia at *Cahiers* was starting to frustrate some editors. A number were eager to reorient the review to serve in a new struggle that ensured *Cahiers* was part of the world it inhabited. This meant acquiring a better understanding of the 'new cinemas' being created around the world, and confronting the downturn of Hollywood *auteurs*; it also meant rethinking the discretion the magazine had shown when dealing with its own sub-products—the New Wave. To some, the concepts developed in the 1950s were not adequate to meet these tasks. Between 1959 and 1966 the chief editor changed three times: a sign of the uncertainty, as well as the continued vitality, of the *Cahiers* project after the victory of the yellow years.

Eric Rohmer's taste for beauty

When in 1958 Bazin died tragically from cancer at the age of forty, Rohmer stepped into the role. He was of the same generation as Bazin, but had always been regarded as a not-so-young Turk. In 1958 he was thirty-seven, and an established writer. Arriving at *Cahiers*, his initial orientation had been more literary than pedagogic or cinematic. By the time the magazine appeared he had published a novel and written several screenplays, as well as introducing films at cine-clubs and editing *Gazette*. Rohmer was also the most available to take over the editor's role: his own directorial career had not taken off in the spectacular fashion of those of his younger colleagues.[34]

---

34 Rohmer's first feature film, made in 1959, was a critical and commercial failure. *The Sign of Leo* was not a typical New Wave film in terms of technique or narrative: rather than hitting the streets with the dynamism and obvious technical audacity of Truffaut or Godard, Rohmer offered an aesthetically sober and poised morality tale. His wandering protagonist plods through the city; a solo violin score is often used instead of dialogue; we visit Neuilly and stay close to the riverbanks, rather than mingling in the cafés, at the

In comparison to the eirenic Bazin, Rohmer was both more mannered and more conservative, writing of Hollywood, for example:

> for the talented and dedicated film-maker the California coast is not the den of iniquity that some would have us believe. It is rather that chosen land, that haven which Florence was for painters of the Quattrocento or Vienna for musicians in the nineteenth century . . . We should love America; and may I add, lest I be reproached with bias, we should love Italy: the Italy of the Roman and the Florentine legacy, but also the capital of Futurist architecture and motor-racing.[35]

In his first decade at *Cahiers* Rohmer had proved himself a formidable critic. His contributions were among the most important on cinema theory in the yellow years, especially his five-part series, 'Celluloid and Marble'. However, the position he elucidated here, in which he sought to understand film based on classical conceptions of art, would come under increasing pressure from old and new members of the *Cahiers* team.

As editor, Rohmer's first challenge was simply to bring in enough material for each issue.[36] With Chabrol, Godard and Truffaut busy making films, and the loss of Bazin, there was a void of capable and inspiring writers. It was at this point that Jean Douchet, a regular on the cine-club circuit, entered the journal. Rohmer quickly allowed Douchet the freedom to pursue his own tastes—Rohmer himself was dividing his attentions between editing and film-making. André Labarthe recalls one day coming to the office before it opened (often not till 6 p.m.!) to find what at first sight appeared to be Rohmer fishing. Half of his long, thin body was hanging outside the window and he was dangling a piece of string. Approaching him, Labarthe

---

pinball machine. Paris was not a playground for fast cars and gun-fights with Rohmer; it was a frustrating and forbidding city, lined and paved with cold stones.

35 *Cahiers* 54, December 1955.

36 The announcement in a small box on the contents page stating that a promised article would be 'in the next issue' became a running joke in the office at the time.

saw that on the end of the string was a microphone: Rohmer was recording the sounds from the kitchen below, with the aim of using the material in a film. This would eventually provide the sound for his first 'moral tale', *The Girl at the Monceau Bakery*, released in 1963.

Jean Douchet was a fervent defender of the classic American *auteurs* and shared many of the tastes of the Mac-Mahonists—a group who took their name from the cinema in Paris that showed only Hollywood films (and had four portraits of the 'masters', Lang, Joseph Losey, Preminger and Raoul Walsh, on its walls). The Mac-Mahonists' passion for these directors' work was taken to the extreme: an unashamed *amour fou*. Rohmer and Douchet allowed the group to articulate their particular liturgy of the gaze in a series of articles published between 1959 and 1962. For many, including Doniol-Valcroze, allowing these critics any space in the magazine was a step towards a right-wing politicization of the *Cahiers* pages. Rumours increased in Paris cinephile circles that the magazine had become an open shop and 'was up for grabs'. The Mac-Mahon controversy split *Cahiers* politically—for the first time. Rohmer and Douchet justified their decision on aesthetic grounds, but their choices excluded modern tendencies such as Buñuel's mockeries of bourgeois mores, or new material from Antonioni—the latter's *L'Eclisse*, for example, considered by Douchet as artifice and nothing but a 'monstrosity'.[37]

Paradoxically, Douchet was also instrumental in recruiting a number of new and talented writers who were keener to pursue these modern tendencies than remain faithful to Losey or Minnelli. Rivette initiated the resistance movement from within, provoked by an article on John Ford's *Two Rode Together*. The issue of racism in the film had been dismissed by the Mac-Mahonist reviewer as 'a kind of provincial snobbism, a pure product of life in society'.[38] Rivette responded by reviewing *Octobre à Paris*: a banned film by former resistance fighter Jacques Panijel, made for the Audin Committee, an organization set up in 1958 following the disappearance of the Algerian mathematician

37 *Cahiers* 132, June 1962.

38 Philippe Hughes, *Cahiers* 127, January 1962.

Maurice Audin. Panijel's film, made with the help of the FLN, amassed as much evidence as possible to prove that Audin had been tortured to death by the French army. By covering it in *Cahiers*, Rivette made a clear political statement of solidarity with the liberation struggle. The film was important because it drew attention to a recent event that had received little attention, compared to the public outcry against the death of eight French protesters at Charonne metro in February 1962. *Octobre à Paris* recorded an earlier protest during which an estimated 200 Algerians had died, some drowning in the Seine after police charges.

Rivette was protesting the editorial decision to publish such a casual endorsement of racism as the *Two Rode Together* review. In response, he praised *Octobre à Paris* as an 'irreplaceable testimony of the condition of North Africans in France, and on their struggle during the winter 1961–62 . . . a document of primary importance for the history of our age'. This was the first time the journal had addressed the issue of the Algerian war. It was the closest *Cahiers* had yet come to articulating a political position.

Two stars for Breathless

Changes were underway at the journal in every respect. *Cahiers* had become a place of passage, its old *chapelle* dispersed as members had left to make films. It lacked a clear source of inspiration: the Mac-Mahonists had demonstrated the upshot of an overly slavish approach to Hollywood. *Cahiers*' wider critical re-evaluation, from *maudit* to iconoclastic, seemed to have run its course. It was at this troubled point, just as its agenda was beginning to waver, that the economic and institutional status of *Cahiers* solidified. By 1960, 12,000 issues were being sold a month, on top of a massive demand for numbers 1 to 100. Regular subscribers stood at 4,000, including 500 universities in the US and Canada. The journal's early ideas were beginning to resonate—and be attacked—in the Anglophone world. The main reason for this was the astonishing originality of the films its erstwhile editors were now creating.

Yet the initial reception of the New Wave at *Cahiers* itself was a bumpy one: no major article appeared on the films in the two years following the explosion of the movement, with the exception of Luc

Moullet's reflective piece on Godard. Jean Domarchi brushed aside *Breathless*, giving it a measly two stars. The first concerted effort to understand and analyse the movement in detail came in December 1962, when a special issue was finally devoted to it. Rohmer had been accused by other writers at *Cahiers* of delaying the issue's publication. His reticence was the result of a certain discretion on his part, and a concern that *Cahiers* would become a mere organ of the New Wave, exposing itself to accusations of nepotism or a *politique des amitiés*—sure to destroy the review's hard-won reputation.[39] Rohmer's editorial for the special issue was candid: as a critic he found it very difficult to place himself outside a movement of which he was part. 'Lacking the truth, let's give it *our* truth: people will take it for what it is worth, but we believe it is a truth that others should not be indifferent to knowing'.

The New Wave also presented *Cahiers* with a different challenge. As an artistic movement in the process of inventing itself, it required a new critical approach, rather than *Cahiers*' previous process of canonizing hitherto ignored *auteurs*. Hitchcock or Hawks offered a body of work made within the industry, and subject to constraints of narrative and conventions of style and genre. Critics could analyse their work as a whole and follow through the recurrent themes. With Truffaut or Godard, however, the same method could not be applied. The New Wave was full of internal contradictions, and operated independently of studios. Rivette conceded that pronouncing a verdict on any contemporary work was very difficult: 'one begins by superimposing the film one expected, which one wanted to see, and even which one wanted to make oneself'.[40]

To make matters more difficult, there were a number of allegedly 'New Wave' films coming out of France that were made by directors to whom *Cahiers* was completely opposed. René Clément's *Plein Soleil*—an adaptation of Patricia Highsmith's *The Talented Mr Ripley*—shared personnel and many techniques with more 'authentic' New Wave films. Paul Gégauff, who wrote Clément's screenplay, was a friend and

39 The term is used by Jean-André Fieschi in *Cahiers 137*, November 1962.

40 Rohmer, *Cahiers* 138, December 1962; Rivette, *Sight and Sound*, Autumn 1963.

collaborator of Rohmer and Chabrol; Henri Decae, who worked the lights, was the operator for Jean-Pierre Melville and Truffaut. *Plein Soleil* was a film about the ultimate act of imitation: Ripley would start by mastering his friend's signature and copying his voice, then he would kill him and literally step into his shoes. Clément was playing a similar game: a director appropriating the New Wave style almost perfectly. *Cahiers* struggled to shoot the film down and expose it as a fraud; only Moullet and Hoveyda used Clément as a counter-example in their articles on Godard and Nicholas Ray. For Moullet, whilst Clément's technique was often the same as Godard's, there was a greater purpose and precise meaning involved in letting the camera in *Breathless* 'roll and roll and roll, always in tempo with the mind of the protagonist . . . It is a very classical expression of modern behaviour'. Hoveyda in turn explored how technique could become either transformative or vacant, depending on the director. Contrasting Clément with Ray, he argued that Clément's close-ups were completely unjustified—and in *Plein Soleil* there are many, particularly the pointless cuts between Alain Delon's face and the swordfish on the Sicilian market stalls. These close-ups showed nothing of what the actors were thinking and might be capable of expressing.[41] Separating the *qualité française* from Bresson or Rossellini had been one thing; now, the task was to distinguish New Wave copycats from their vastly superior models. Critical demolitions were called for, requiring new critical tools, and this would occupy *Cahiers*' writers throughout the sixties.

New Wave trough

The silence at *Cahiers* around the New Wave was particularly vexing for the young directors, because they desperately needed the magazine's support. Audiences had flocked to see the first films by Truffaut and Chabrol, *The 400 Blows* and *Le Beau Serge*—450,000 and 416,000 spectators respectively—but their following releases were comparatively less successful: 100,000 for *Shoot the Pianist*; 53,000 for *Wise Guys*. Many critics at other publications remained unconvinced.

41 *Cahiers* 106, April 1960; *Cahiers* 107, May 1960.

Roger Tailleur at *Positif* was as unimpressed by the New Wave's engagement with politics and philosophy as by their experimental techniques. He felt the work of the young directors was merely an escape into formalism. Their films betrayed 'fear' when treating more difficult subjects, which 'generates feverish diversion tactics. As soon as people touch on deep and serious matters they take refuge in everyday banality and platitudes. Everything is seen in terms of stage tricks, with reassuring winks to the audience, claims that none of this really matters. The mental vacuity within a speech is disguised by a sprinkling of references to book titles, the odd quote from Gorky, attributed, for even greater effect, to Lenin . . . under the guise of anarchy we find utterly mindless immobility, mental hibernation.'[42]

The New Wave directors also received little help from the state via Malraux's innovative *avances sur recettes*. The proclaimed goal of this sponsoring system was to assist young French cinema by granting advances on the presentation of a script, rather than rewarding the finished work. However, the system tended to select conservative features over anything experimental. The improvisational style of Truffaut or Godard with their careful attention to *mise en scène* and camerawork were not qualities evident on paper, whereas familiar and wordier literary adaptations appeared immediately more promising. The advance system always favoured the projects it felt it could assess prior to realization. Truffaut, Godard, Chabrol, Rohmer and Rivette received nothing before 1965; only after the New Wave movement was over did Godard (1965), Rohmer (1967) and Truffaut (1968) receive any aid, while Rivette got no funds at all throughout the sixties. It was a handful of maverick, risk-taking producers that enabled many New Wave films to be made, not the *avance sur recettes*.[43]

Mounting an offensive

The opposition to the Rohmerian line solidified initially with the 'group of five': Doniol-Valcroze, Godard, Kast, Truffaut and

42 Roger Tailleur, 'Le Roi est nu', *Positif* 46, June 1962.

43 René Prédal, *50 Ans du cinéma français*, Paris 1996, pp. 262–5.

Rivette. They wanted him to reorient the review towards a more open engagement with new currents in cinema and culture. But for Rohmer it was not the world that ever changed, 'only art'. He saw cinema flourishing creatively, whereas the other arts were in a period of decadence.[44] Classicism in cinema was not something in the past, it belonged to the here and now:

> cinema does not make monsters out of planes, cars, phones and guns . . . it shows them as they are in everyday life, just like the bows and arrows or the galleons of the ancient world; they seem to be part and parcel of their surroundings, at one with the hand that moves and directs them. The intention which lay behind their original creation appears to inhabit them still. The way they move recreates and enhances immeasurably the noble gesture of man who first conceived them.[45]

Rohmer was first invited to make some changes himself that could enable *Cahiers* to once again become an instrument of struggle. But his subsequent text, 'The Taste for Beauty', was a striking articulation of the editorial line as he saw it. Rohmer was proud of the stability the journal enjoyed under his leadership. His preference for small budgets and sparse resources—which he would carry through into his work as a director—was established at *Cahiers* and he saw no need to change it. On the contrary, the magazine had become the 'cinephiles' journal', a key part of their critical consciousness and a real reference for all those involved in film culture. As editor, Rohmer held true to the publication's original aim of establishing film as the seventh art. He was not interested in militancy, or in focusing upon the latest innovations of modern cinema. Rather, he believed that 'the clearest aim in our struggle, one which we have every intention of leading in the coming years', must be to set down the foundations for 'cinema museums' around the world. He was determined, in other words, to enable film to be

---

44 *Cahiers* 172, November 1965. Rohmer must however be credited with first bringing Brecht to the journal, publishing Bernard Dort's 'Pour une critique brechtienne du cinéma', *Cahiers* 114, December 1960.
45 *Cahiers* 121, July 1961.

considered by future generations under a museum optic. At *Cahiers* under Rohmer, critics should 'nourish the ambitious aim of judging *sub specie aeternitatis'*—under the aspect of eternity.[46]

But this was no longer a cause the group of five wanted to rally around. Rohmer's reticence towards the New Wave was one point of contention; his reluctance to address much modern cinema was eventually impossible to accept. For the first time, political disagreements aggravated the aesthetic discord: the preference for Losey and Minnelli over Antonioni and Buñuel signified for the group of five a conservative, even right-wing position.

Rivette's putsch

Rivette was the leading figure who charged Rohmer with allowing a *confort de caste*, or complacency of thought, to set in that left *Cahiers* isolated from the dynamic present. He wanted to attend to alternative sources of innovation. New cinema from Europe (Bertolucci, Pasolini, the Polish 'workshops'), Brazilian *cinema nôvo* and Direct Cinema from around the world began to be addressed. Rejecting pure cinephilia, he sought an opening of the journal to broader intellectual movements. After the failed attempts by Truffaut and Doniol-Valcroze in 1962 to encourage Rohmer to reassess some of the old *Cahiers* tenets, Rivette mounted an alternative team. The end of Rohmer's reign was undignified for a man of such elegance in writing and directing. It was also cruel. He put together number 144 at the same time as Rivette's competing team worked on their issue, and, in a lonely final flurry, wrapped up his version in his pyjamas after a white night at the office. It was published, but it was to be his last. Rivette had the support of the editorial board and, by now, of most of the contributing critics. *Cahiers* 145 announced the change of editors: Rivette was at the head and Rohmer out the door.[47]

46 Rohmer, *Cahiers* 121, July 1961.

47 Reflecting on this 'putsch' today, many of those who were part of Rivette's group admit that whilst they believe it was absolutely necessary—*Cahiers* would have perished otherwise; it was too detached and there were many sub-standard contributors being allowed to write for the review—they regret the harsh manner of its execution. Rohmer too, though reticent

In his first editorial in August 1963, Rivette responded immediately to the problem Godard had raised in his 1962 interview: what had made *Cahiers* was 'its position in the front line of battle', but with everyone now largely in agreement with *Cahiers*' arguments, 'there isn't so much to say'. Positions that had been high stakes in the fifties had become 'dogma and system', Rivette reiterated, and criticism had to evolve. The postures that had been adopted 'from a tactical point of view' were now *caducs*—clapped-out.[48] Later he would describe how the experience of watching his *Paris Belongs to Us* in a crowded cinema in 1960 had changed his notions of film criticism: it had to consider the context in which films were made and seen. The cinephile approach, too awestruck by the screen, precluded this.

> Such are the perils of the 'pure gaze' attitude that leads one to complete submission before a film . . . like cows in a field transfixed by the sight of passing trains, but with little hope of ever understanding what makes them move.[49]

Engaging with the changing social landscape of which film was a part, both in its production and its reception, meant a break with the old agenda. Cinema could not be understood in isolation and, most importantly, it need not be. *Cahiers*' first ten years had laid the foundation for taking film seriously; now criticism had to grasp the new points of tension.

Cinema's Copernican revolution

The opening that characterized Rivette's editorship between 1963 and 1965 involved a new receptivity to other disciplines and

---

on the subject to this day, remains deeply hurt by the way *Cahiers* treated him. The putsch did, however, free Rohmer to dedicate himself entirely to film-making, and with the aid of Barbet Schroeder—who played the lead in Rohmer's first 'moral tale'—he set up a production company, Films du Losange, in 1962. Given the œuvre that has subsequently followed, one is indeed thankful that the putsch took place.

48 *Cahiers* 172, November 1965.

49 *Cahiers* 146, August 1963.

intellectual currents: anthropology, literary theory and, a little later, the psychoanalysis of Lacan and concepts of ideology developed by Althusser. All were brought to bear on understanding the nature of cinema as a twentieth-century art form. Rivette was inspired by the array of new styles and visions emanating from the other arts. Abstract Expressionism had arrived in Paris via exhibitions by Jackson Pollock in 1959 and Mark Rothko in 1962; music, too, was exploring new forms, with Pierre Boulez's Domaine musical concerts, Schoenberg's *Moses and Aaron*, and the works of Webern, Berg and Stockhausen. Modern cinema, Rivette went so far as to say, was musical. In February 1964 a full section in *Cahiers* was devoted to the soundtrack alone. Whereas the *politique* had been established through long conversations with practicing *auteurs*, the new masters to be invited to face a *Cahiers* interrogation were drawn from outside the cinematic environment. As well as Roland Barthes, Claude Lévi-Strauss and Pierre Boulez, Jean-Paul Sartre was invited for interview, though he declined.

Bazin's maxim, 'cinema is a language', was re-examined within the linguistic paradigms of structuralism. This approach conceived of film as containing codes and modes of expression that worked according to the same mechanism as signs and syntax. Such codes permitted meaning to exist in films, but were communicated in various and complex ways, which the concept of *mise en scène* was deemed too vague to fully explain. Alternatives were proposed, such as Pasolini's long text in 1965 describing a nascent 'poetic cinema' that would be the maturation of neo-realism; the rejection of conventional narrative 'prose' and the use of ellipses in the work of Antonioni or Resnais made interpretation essential, almost to the point of erasing the significance of the *auteur*. Interviewed by *Cahiers*, Barthes affirmed that 'man is so fatally bound to meaning that freedom in art might seem to consist . . . not so much in creating meaning as suspending it'.[50] Resnais's *Last Year in Marienbad* had marked a 'Copernican revolution' for *Cahiers* critics. As with modernist painting, where 'the task of the painter is no longer to paint a subject, but to make a canvas',

50 *Cahiers* 147, September 1963; *Cahiers* 123, September 1961.

so with the camera: 'the film-maker's job is no longer to tell a story, but simply to make a film in which the spectator will discover a story'. The audience was now becoming 'the hero of the film'.[51] Bresson's *Au hasard Balthazar* was celebrated for its economy of signification and its subtractive quality:

> [he] wants each image to express only what he wants to make it express, after eliminating what one might call 'noise' . . . he is forced to resort to a style that eliminates inevitably ambiguous facial expressions, too loaded with meaning . . . Ellipsis becomes obligatory, because he cannot dwell too long on any one face.[52]

A review of Buñuel's *Belle de jour* made clear the new critical tools being employed. The article was saturated with structuralist language: 'the film is articulated through two formal series which must be read in abstraction from any "level" or "hierarchy" '.[53] Jean-Louis Comolli, in an early contribution to the journal, confirmed his transition from Rohmerian to Rivettian attitudes: citing Blanchot, Heidegger, Merleau-Ponty and Jung, he proposed a relationship between philosophy and cinema, a way of feeling the film by thinking it. New work should aim not to lull its audience with the comfort of ritual within the darkened auditorium, but to unsettle and provoke greater reflection.[54] Rivette, too, welcomed such disturbance: 'the role of cinema is to destroy myths . . . to take people out of their cocoons'.[55]

The new works by Federico Fellini, Miklós Jancsó, Jean-Marie Straub, Godard and Tati were among the strongest examples of this 'cinema of signification', being understood through a Barthesian perspective. They all reconstituted the relationship to narrative within the film, and consequently changed the engagement of the audience with the fiction. 'A film is always presented in a closed

51 François Weyergans, *Cahiers* 123, September 1961; Jean-Louis Comolli, *Cahiers* 177, April 1966.

52 André Labarthe, in a round table on the film, *Cahiers* 180, July 1966.

53 Jean Narboni, *Cahiers* 192, July–August 1967.

54 *Cahiers* 141 and 143, March and May 1963.

55 *Cahiers* 204, September 1968.

form', Rivette would later explain. It is a certain number of reels, screened in a particular order. However, within this exist any number of circulating meanings, functions and forms which can remain unresolved. This incompleteness was, for Rivette, the real strength of modern cinema and what directors should aim to achieve: a film or a work should not exhaust its coherence, close in on itself; 'it must continue to function, and to create new meanings, directions and feelings.'[56]

The next generation

Under Rivette's editorship, the keynote articles being published were by the new generation of cinephiles drawn into the *Cahiers* orbit in the early sixties. Ironically, since these would be the critics behind the putsch, many had been invited to write for the review by Jean Douchet (who also had to leave when Rivette took over). Omnipresent on the Parisian cine-club scene, Douchet met many young cinephiles and budding critics whom he encouraged to write for *Cahiers*. Among the most influential arrivals were two medical students from Algeria: Jean-Louis Comolli (b. 1937) and Jean Narboni (b. 1941). Both men had cut their teeth at the Ciné-club d'Alger before coming to Paris to study in 1961. Another new arrival was Serge Daney (b. 1944). A *Cahiers* reader since the age of fifteen, while still a teenager Daney had started his own short-lived film journal, *Visages du cinéma*, with his friend and fellow-devotee Louis Skorecki. Unprecedented for *Cahiers*, the latter two were adventurous travellers and their early contributions were as roving critics, reporting back from India, Africa and America. Bernard Eisenschitz was a Russian and German specialist, and helped to fill a much-needed hole in *Cahiers*' coverage of these cinemas when he arrived in 1967. Michel Delahaye was a student of Lévi-Strauss and admirer of Jean Rouch's ethnographic cinema. *Nouveau roman* author Claude Ollier and critic Jean-André Fieschi—who was close friends with Comolli and Jean Eustache—also came aboard, Fieschi embracing an avant-garde ethic that rejected the 'illusory explication

56 *Cahiers* 323–324, May–June 1981.

of beauty' of the *mise en scène*.[57] All were equipped with a broader range of theoretical interests, and in contrast to the yellow years, a number would remain critics, as opposed to evolving into critics–*cinéastes* as the previous cohort had.

This new crop subsequently discarded the whole notion of *mise en scène*, much as abstract painters had done away with figuration. Initially, the *mise en scène* had been invoked as a reaction against the critical tendency to talk exclusively in terms of themes and subjects, emphasizing the idea that cinema is also something which one sees on the screen. It provided a means of understanding film as the expression of a specifically personal vision. By the sixties, the consensus at *Cahiers* was that the concept had been abused to the point of nonsense. Echoing the early reservations of André Bazin in 1953, when he argued that Huston's *The Red Badge of Courage* was far better than either *Strangers on a Train* or *Rope* because 'the subject also counts for something', Rivette complained that *mise en scène* was 'now used to suggest that as long as the camera movement can be called sublime, it makes no difference if the story is fatuous, the dialogue idiotic and the acting atrocious.'[58] Labarthe called for the end of *mise en scène* as a concept, finding it debilitating for current critics who had become 'victims' and 'prisoners' of their own language.[59]

Turning on the lights

What critics were now expected to grasp were the external elements: the act of contextualizing a work was paramount; the sense of what environment a film had come out of, its connection with the world, and

57 Fieschi, *Cahiers* 172, November 1965.

58 Bazin acknowledged that Hitchcock certainly had a personal style and was the inventor of original cinematographic forms, 'and in this sense his superiority over Huston is incontestable'. Yet Bazin chose *The Red Badge of Courage* over the last two films by the Englishman because Huston treated the subject matter with superior intelligence and subtlety. There were no formal innovations, but Huston's great achievement was to 'interiorize cinematographic expression to the point of erasing the spectacle'. *Cahiers* 27, October 1953; Rivette in interview with *Sight and Sound*, Autumn 1963.

59 *Cahiers* 195, November 1967.

its expression of this. National cinemas were singled out as objects of study; from each film was extrapolated the particular economic, social and political conditions out of which it had emerged, and its entire production history was tracked. Out with the *esprit de Cinémathèque*, where bodies and minds were shut away from the outside world; it was time for the lights to come on. Godard characterized the shift accordingly:

> The approach to criticism ten years ago was like Mendeleev's classification of the elements: everyone thought there were seven or eight of them and the New Wave claimed there were far more than that, two hundred or three hundred. And from that point onwards, modern chemistry was born.[60]

Rohmer had traced the shift from 'marble to celluloid', but with a view to make cinema part of the musuem. The transformation Godard described was more dramatic. Modern cinema was unpredictable, capricious, open to freer interpretation, and its criticism had to adjust. Interesting and innovative work was also to be found elsewhere. By the mid-sixties, the *auteurs* that *Cahiers*' Hitchcocko-Hawksians had spotlighted within Hollywood were growing old and disappointing their fans with their later works—Ray's *55 Days at Peking*, Hawks's *Man's Favourite Sport*, Ford's *Cheyenne Autumn*, Preminger's *Exodus* and *In Harm's Way*, Hitchcock's *Torn Curtain*. The cinematic horizon had expanded to India (Satyajit Ray), Japan (Kurosawa), Brazil (Rocha); Czechoslovakia (Milos Forman, Jan Svankmajer), Poland (Polanski, Wajda), the USSR (Tarkovsky), Germany (Danièlle Huillet and Jean-Marie Straub), Sweden (Bergman), Italy (Antonioni, Fellini, Pasolini) and within France itself (Buñuel, Marker, Resnais, Rouch).

Working with cine-clubs, in 1966 *Cahiers* introduced a new international section, covering the latest releases from around the world. Comolli welcomed the advent of a new political cinema in which one could see 'the sharp point of a struggle which is not only

60 *Cahiers* 171, October 1965.

artistic but which involves a society, a morality, a civilization'.[61] To understand these, the triangle of film–public–*auteur* had to be broken. Originally the New Wave had based its success on reaching as wide an audience as possible, because this marked the distribution of a work of art, and not just *qualité française*. But audiences had been in decline since the start of the sixties. The appetite for New Wave films decreased rapidly, and mass viewing of the moving image was shifting progressively to television. New films from around the world did not always have a popular touch or a global reach. At *Cahiers* this was immaterial—it was believed the films could find their public later. This shift in the *Cahiers* position vis-à-vis the public made it far more wary of the mainstream—the interesting works were moving to, being increasingly forced to, the margins. Innovation and creativity would more likely be found outside the system than within it.

Multicoloured Cahiers

In 1964 *Cahiers*' publisher, Editions de l'Etoile, was bought by Daniel Filipacchi, best known as the entrepreneur behind the magazine and radio programme *Salut les copains*. He owned a number of other titles that catered to the youth and male market, such as *Mademoiselle age tendre*, *Lui*, *Playboy* and *Penthouse*.[62] His arrival was a bitter pill for editors to swallow, and a major factor in Godard's long split from *Cahiers* that took effect from 1967. Filipacchi did not, however, impose many demands on *Cahiers* editorially, beyond indulging his penchant for reproducing flashy film stills. In the same year as Filipacchi's arrival, *Cahiers* underwent its first major redesign, though this reflected the intellectual shifts of the journal more than managerial changes. The famous yellow cover was replaced by a different colour each month, and by 1966 the black-and-white *coup de cœur*—the arresting image that always fronted the issue—was also in

61 *Cahiers* 176, March 1966.

62 Filipacchi has remained a pivotal figure in the French magazine market. In 1976 he turned around the fortunes of a then-ailing *Paris-match;* in 1981 he teamed up with businessman and Saint-Simonian Jean-Luc Lagardère to form Hachette Filipacchi Magazines.

colour. It is significant that the comfortable familiarity of the *Cahiers jaunes* was an immediate target for the new team. The refusal to allow its readers the recognizable symbol of old-style cinephilia was an active expression of the growing critique of that culture within the journal's pages, an internal purging of golden-ageism. Rivette's takeover had been decisive, but the classicism of his predecessor had given way to a series of questions, rather than a definable alternative line. To some extent the very diversity of the new editorial team reflected this: a mix of travellers, doctors, novelists, anthropologists. The form of the journal became protean, the size of the issues expanding to fifty, seventy, eighty, and even two hundred pages in December 1963; yet sales remained stable, at 15,000 copies a month throughout the sixties.

In October 1964, a still from Antonioni's *The Red Desert* adorned the final yellow cover. A shot from the same film was on the front of the next issue, but this time Monica Vitti—seen beside the car rather than inside it—was framed by a striking shade of orange. It was fitting that *The Red Desert* should close the yellow years, and open the new format. Antonioni's work represented the extreme point of modern cinema, and it was exactly the kind of film that had split the editorial group in the run up to Rivette's putsch. Comolli explained the significance of the film in a review that could be taken as a prologue to the next editorial cycle awaiting *Cahiers*. *The Red Desert* was about this world, but it asked us to look at it again. Antonioni 'tells us that we know only what has already been understood, and we live in the already not understood. We walk with our own portable oasis through the desert, but what we believe to be that oasis is a desert, and the desert is an oasis.'[63] A far more complicated world of possibility had opened up that could not be expressed through loyalty to the *auteur* alone. Editors would dispense with the comfortable precepts of Mendeleev's classification of the elements and walk towards an exhilarating, multicoloured future.

63 *Cahiers* 159, October 1964.

John Cassavetes, *Faces* (1968)

4

1966–1969
Politicization

Jean-Louis Comolli and Jean Narboni were chosen by Rivette to replace him at the head of the magazine in 1965. Having steered *Cahiers* in the direction he believed necessary, Rivette quickly vacated the editor role to concentrate on making his new film, *La Religieuse*. He did however remain a very important influence, dropping by the office all the time, pronouncing, with the same absolute authority and explosive passion—he had a 'chemical reaction' to films, Jean-André Fieschi remembers—his judgement on the latest releases.

Shortly following their accession, the new co-editor team organized a round-table to take stock of *Cahiers*' critical concepts such as the old *politique des auteurs* and re-evaluate American cinema 'twenty years on'. Bazin had never been convinced by the *politique*, because it was a policy more than a theory and only succeeded when it was conducted by 'people of taste'. The main purveyors of aesthetic value were now busy behind their own movie cameras, and Comolli and Narboni drew blunt conclusions: the *politique* at *Cahiers* had been expanded and distorted. It produced slippages and confusions, finally 'stretching [the policy] to the point where the *auteur* and his subject matter endow each other with a mutual value'. The criteria for being an *auteur* were too weak: 'even the worst film-makers have their obsessions', and failed to qualify only because they dealt with these fixations heavy-handedly rather than creatively.[64]

64 *Cahiers* 172, November 1965.

The gathering at this round-table to mark the mid-point of the decade was the first occasion at which tried and tested formulas were self-consciously reconsidered with the aim of developing a more rigorous theory, rather than the vague, non-transferable quality of taste. It brought no immediate breakthroughs. Critic Michel Mardore—who also dabbled in acting, with bit-parts in Rohmer's *Girl at the Monceau Bakery* and Jacques Demy's *Donkey's Skin*—only offered a regression on the magazine's previous position: 'we don't have the right to lay down the law, elevate one form over another, we have to defend the notion of a pluralism of styles against a desiccated classicism'.[65] Nor did Comolli or Narboni broaden their considerations to inquire into the industry, economic conditions or political conjuncture. However, over the next four years this vacillation and vagueness, and especially the distance from politics would be completely overturned, culminating in the editorial-manifesto of 1969: 'Cinema/Ideology/Criticism', that set out *Cahiers*' line with scientific precision.

Struggling on two fronts

The year 1966 proved the key political turning point. France's boom years, *les trente glorieuses* were culminating in rapid modernization, and the country experienced an influx of modern technology, from fridges and television sets to motor cars.[66] But under the cloud of the Vietnam War, America no longer appeared to be an innocent ally in the depiction of the lights and shadows of modernity. Its impact on French life was being registered ever more sourly. Jacques Tati's comedies turned increasingly bleak and he had his enormous set for *Playtime* destroyed after the film's completion—the project had cost Tati his fortune and reputation, but still he refused to turn it for profit into a theme park or museum, as some had suggested. Instead his vanguard act stood against the bureaucratization and monotonous excess of modern life that the set had represented. Simone de Beauvoir

---

65 *Cahiers* 172, November 1965.

66 In 1958, 9 per cent of households owned a TV; by the end of the sixties this was up to 60 per cent. For a cultural account and critical approach, see Kristin Ross, *Fast Cars, Clean Bodies*, Cambridge, MA 1995.

distilled with acid prose in her novel, *Les Belles images*, the prevailing mindset of the *France-Dimanche* generation whose heads were filled with magazine marketing slogans and lives progressively retreating into the comfortable but alienating interiors of their cars and homes.

Worldwide, tremendous popular energies were unleashed in the national liberation struggles in Indo-China, Africa and Latin America and in the Krushchevite thaw in Eastern Europe. At the same time was the mass upsurge of the Cultural Revolution in China, where a Communist leader was beseeching the young to bombard governmental headquarters with their criticisms, abolish the difference between manual and intellectual labour and between peasant and town-dweller, and to re-vitalize the revolution. With a nod to Che, Godard summed up the new, specifically cinematic perspective in his press release for *La Chinoise* the following year:

> The American industry rules cinema the world over. There is nothing much to add to this statement of fact. Except that on our own modest level we too should provoke two or three Vietnams in the bosom of the vast Hollywood–Cinecittà–Mosfilm–Pinewood empire, and, both economically and aesthetically, struggling on two fronts as it were, create cinemas which are national, free, fraternal, comradely and bonded in friendship.[67]

At home, the chafing of an arrogant and authoritarian Gaullist state was becoming intolerable. French censorship had previously applied

67 Godard's politicization came at the hands of his young girlfriend, Anne Wiazemsky, whom he had first seen as the seventeen-year-old star of Bresson's *Au hasard Balthazar*. Studying at Nanterre, she introduced him to student circles electrified by the discovery of Marx's 1844 manuscripts, liberation psychology and the pill. Godard cast Wiazemsky as the lead in *La Chinoise*, an ambivalent portrayal of youth radicalization that both endorses a Maoist politics and predicts its decline. The young students, doing their exercises every morning while chanting party slogans, are right in their critique but fatally isolated from the world outside. See Colin MacCabe, *Godard: A Portrait of the Artist at 70*, London 2003, chapter 4; and for the first meeting between the two, Anne Wiazemsky, *Jeune fille*, Paris 2007, pp. 192–8.

the scissors to New Wave films; footage of Eisenhower and De Gaulle had to be cut from *Breathless*, for example. But the banning of Rivette's *La Religieuse* in 1966 for its anti-clericalism was a brutal awakening for the *Cahiers* team—as Anna Karina's suffering face on the cover of issue 177 evoked. Comolli and Narboni started to tilt from post-structuralism to a more declamatory militancy. In his March 1966 editorial, Comolli shifted the critical attention from issues of style or aesthetics to those of working conditions, economic structures and technical requirements. He argued that it was in these domains that the New Wave had truly revolutionized activity. They had transformed 'a certain conception of the entertainment industry' and their working practice was inspiring young film-makers internationally—the movement proved to emerging directors such as Rainer Werner Fassbinder in Germany, Jerzy Skolimowski in Poland or Jancsó in Hungary that films gaining worldwide attention could be made even on a shoestring budget with little backing and a small team.

Cahiers still covered the latest releases from ageing *auteurs* working in the debris of the old studio system, but without the passion and loyalty that the old *politique des auteurs* had produced. Editors prioritized engagement with the 'new cinema', and this required an end to the lingering detachment from politics and the world. An editorial statement in August 1966 duly announced the end of the 'Council of Ten' ratings for new releases: 'cinema has increasingly less resemblance to the image created by the kinds of films shown on the Champs-Elysées, or even in the Latin Quarter', it determined; henceforth, of the films released in Paris 'we intend to discuss only those which merit attention—or stricture'. Discussion of these 'minor' films dominated *Cahiers* from the latter half of 1966 onwards; a rubric entitled 'Situation of the New Cinema' became a permanent fixture in each issue.

Whilst the term 'new cinema' was vague, potentially designating anything from any country around the world and encompassing an array of styles, the impulse that gave the concept coherence was primarily political: 'each [new cinema film] finds itself at the sharp point of a struggle which is not only artistic but which involves a society, a morality, a civilization: cinemas of the revolution'. The new cinema also demanded a rather different activity from the critic than had hitherto been practised. In his hectoring editorial of November 1967, 'Why? Where? How? When?' Comolli's tone had grown ominous: critics must 'go down into the arena', their writing should be 'compromised and implicated up to the neck in work being done now'. Their task was not 'to make the dead speak', or 'rifle the pockets of corpses', but rather 'to finish off the dying in the field of battle'. As a result, criticism would become 'more dangerous' and 'more present'.[68] In an interview the same year, Godard stressed the change of location which applied to directors too: 'We have to draw up a list of places where [cinema] does not exist yet and tell ourselves—that is where we have to go. If it isn't in the factories, we shall take it there. If it isn't in the universities, we shall enter the universities. If it isn't in the brothels, we shall go to the brothels. Cinema has to leave the places where it exists and go wherever it does not'.[69]

New Wave fraudsters

Given this combative role, which ensured that the neglected films of the new cinema were at least covered in *Cahiers*, editors tended towards laudatory rather than negative criticism: better to champion work they admired and supported than waste time on poor films with wide distribution. There was no pandering to popular taste if editors disagreed with the choices of audiences.

The journal did not confine itself to eulogies, however, and the crowd-pleasing Claude Lelouch provoked a major *Cahiers* offensive against his purported New Wave style of cinema. *A Man and a Woman* had been a glittering success when it came out in 1966. Audiences went to see it en masse, making it the second-highest grossing film of the year; critics loved it too, presenting Lelouch with the Palme d'Or at Cannes in May. In response, Comolli demolished the film and dismissed Lelouch's claims that he was part of the New Wave simply because he directed, wrote, produced and filmed his own features. In

---

68 *Cahiers* 195, November 1967.

69 *Cahiers* 194, October 1967.

a devastating attack that set down the strong editorial line, Comolli unravelled the 'layers of fakery' in *A Man and a Woman*. It represented a 'risk-proof way of retrieving the formal mannerisms of modern cinema, the tinsel of modernity whose soul has been removed'. In his use of improvisation, music, ellipses, tricks of sound and use of quotations, Lelouch was the polar opposite of a New Wave director. The film's 'incoherence and disorder' were not the effects of art, but 'the clinical symptom of a pathological incapacity to choose, eliminate, decide—to direct.' Bresson, Renoir or Rossellini described directing as 'suppressing', 'aiming at the essential'; Lelouch's proliferating images, on the contrary, 'are a disease of cinema, its cancer'.

Comolli also addressed the underlying reason for the fashionable success of the film by explaining that it gave the Champs-Elysées crowd a 'clear conscience'—in other words, it gave them nothing at all. Comolli was resigned to the fact that a 'cinema of ideas and questions, the modern cinema, is never going to do well there.' By comparison, Comolli praised Godard's films for intentionally making people uncomfortable. Godard's 'challenge to the language of cinema, and the world through that language and the language of that world through cinema . . . irritates because it runs contrary to people's usual experience' and their 'comfortable view of the world'. Lelouch offered only 'fragmentation' and 'frenzy' but no reflection. It was as though Godard's dystopian *Alphaville* had arrived, where 'conscience', 'why' and 'love' are forgotten words. So, Lelouch's film was 'comprehensible and accessible to everyone. Because there is nothing to understand—just help yourself to what you want.'[70]

Looking at you

The audience had become a distinct object of critical analysis in April 1966, with Comolli's 'Notes on the New Spectator'. In the Lelouch polemic, he treated the punters with a mixture of disparagement—the trendy Champs-Elysées crowd would never accept modern cinema—and flattery, criticizing Lelouch above all for being in contempt of

70 *Cahiers* 180, July 1966.

the public by offering such a dumb spectacle, and presenting it as 'simplicity, nature, life'. 'To propose this debilitated cinema first of all means despising the spectator', Comolli argued, 'and the desire to be basic means denying their intelligence. Setting your sights low means aiming at a lower target'.[71] People had flocked to see the film, however, and its popularity should not be brushed aside. Given that cinema could have a transformative effect and encourage social reform, it could just as easily serve as a device for endorsing the dominant ideology. In the case of Lelouch and his very widely seen film, conventions were disseminated and entrenched in society under the aegis of entertainment and art. The million-dollar-smile duo of Jean-Louis Trintignant and Anouk Aimée, captured in jump cuts giggling at each other inside a car or on endless boat trips and walks on the beach, serenaded by a mishmash of classical and contemporary pop, plus a motor-racing subplot in Monte Carlo, all seduced viewers—but what was being conveyed was not innocent: these images sold the dream of bourgeois society. The rich moral ambiguity of old westerns or *noirs* was being replaced with the beautification of consumerism.

A month earlier, in 'Notes on the New Spectator', Comolli had contrasted the tendency of mainstream cinema to underestimate its audience with the form and content being developed in new cinema. The latter, he argued here and in later articles, required an active audience to have its full effect, indeed to be of any worth at all. The new cinema represented an active resistance to the dominant ideology from its conception, production and reception: it 'disturbs the whole mutually tranquilizing producer-consumer osmosis game', Comolli argued.[72] Faced with these films, the role of the spectator was elevated to that of an active subject and the film was imbued with the power to provoke social change. In this sense, Comolli went on, both the making and criticism of films involved 'a political choice to stop seeing the audience as an inert, amorphous mass open to all sorts of manipulation by advertising'. Instead one must 'bank on the existence of an audience that is lucid' and 'ultimately as creative as the film-

71 *Cahiers* 180, July 1966.
72 *Cahiers* 177, April 1966.

maker'. Presenting cinema as 'one of the rare effective means of reform', Comolli justified the talk of politics, not just art, at *Cahiers*. New cinema offered films that 'are no longer the idealizing or realist mirror of the world'; they shook us out of our reverie by 'shattering the mirror itself, revealing the reflection for what it is'.[73]

Art can transform life. It is political. These were the assumptions now underpinning the *Cahiers* project. As directors, Godard, Rivette, Rohmer and Truffaut—all interviewed between 1965 and 1968—had fast become wary of commercial success and to preserve artistic autonomy had tended to accept a compromise: to make films on their own terms meant making cinema for a minority public. It was a major shift from their early aim to suppress the opposition between art films for the few and popular movies for the masses.

As critics, it had been at the heart of their defence of Hitchcock and Hawks; as directors, the aspiration to be seen by as many as possible drove *Breathless* and *Paris Belongs to Us*. The young Turks incorporated melodrama and romance into their first films, and freely took inspiration from detective fictions and *noir* thrillers because these were all seductive ingredients. They were not embarrassed to use them; on the contrary, the most conventional narrative could always be presented in radically fresh ways. The New Wave films would break down any distinction between elite cinema and mainstream entertainment. Instead, there would just be good and bad films; aesthetic value judgements would work along these same lines, and for all types of audiences. But by the mid-sixties this aim had not, in concrete terms, been realized.[74]

---

73 *Cahiers* 190, May 1967.

74 Three Godard films released in 1966—*La Chinoise*, *Two or Three Things I Know about Her* and *Made in USA*—sold no more than 241,000 tickets combined; Robbe-Grillet's *Trans-Europe-Express* brought 93,000 entries; Bresson's *Mouchette* 86,000; Rohmer's *La Collectionneuse*, 52,000. In other words, the entries for the six major art films of the year combined did not even come close to the number of tickets bought for the top two French films of the year: Lelouch's *A Man and a Woman* (708,000) and Gérard Oury's comedy *Don't Look Now—We're Being Shot At* (1,296,000). András Bálint Kovács, *Screening Modernism: European Art Cinema, 1950–1980*, Chicago and London 2007, p. 305. Cinema attendance statistics from *Image et son* 212,

After 1962 the broad popularity of the New Wave rapidly declined, and audience figures increasingly showed a consistent split between art films and genre films, to the benefit of the latter. The success of Lelouch encapsulated the trend. With the majority of spectators going to film theatres in order to see nothing at all, there was a clash between the aesthetic choices at *Cahiers*—new cinema, not always widely seen—and a more politicized project of overturning the consensus and shattering the dominant ideology. Was *Cahiers* now consigned to addressing only a minority public? Had the connection between popular films and high art, via elitist cinephilia, been severed decisively?

Films without a master

Another subject to which critics started to turn their attention was the reconfiguration of the relationship between fiction and documentary evident in much new cinema. Straub and Huillet in Europe; Brazil's *cinema nôvo* led by Glauber Rocha; Fernando Solanas in Argentina—all were offering new ways of thinking about this frontier. In France, Rivette's own work was exploring the documentary form, which he argued involved an even stronger role for the audience. The viewer should be asked to participate in a common work, one that may be 'long' and 'difficult', the viewing experience akin to 'delivering a baby'—but it was cinema's role to contradict the structures that organized people's ideas.[75]

What Rivette also broke with—and what *Cahiers* had hitherto still retained—was the dependence on the director's individual genius in creating such an effective work. Instead, directors should 'deny that film is a personal creation'. What this meant in practice he demonstrated immediately, releasing his four-hour *L'Amour fou* in 1968, the same year that he was interviewed by *Cahiers*. The film convinced the team that his approach was the right one. Sylvie Pierre, the first female critic at *Cahiers* following more than a decade

---

January 1968, p. 82.

75 *Cahiers* 204, September 1968.

with men in charge, and specialist on Brazilian *cinema nôvo*, praised Rivette's film as one 'without a master'. The director had 'aspired not to be God' and has tried instead 'to produce a non-fiction—or rather, a fiction which aims to give such a faithful account of non-fiction modes that it ends up conforming to them'.[76]

The style with which Rivette and others were experimenting became known as 'Direct Cinema'. *Cahiers* devoted much attention to it—Jean Rouch's *cinéma vérité*, long-admired at *Cahiers*, was an important precursor. John Cassavetes was its greatest US exponent, and on the release of the American's second feature *Faces* in 1968, Pierre and Comolli were ecstatic: it was a *chef d'œuvre* of the form. Cassavetes' film was a highly concentrated, fictional account of middle-class American relationships in free-fall that also forced viewers to reflect on the nature of cinema itself. The film 'makes us aware of one of cinema's weaknesses: its inability to explain the inner world, since all it can literally grasp are external signs'. *Faces* successfully merged content with form, borrowing from the effects of alcohol—its heightened awareness and lucidity, moments of emotion and flashes of insight—and using this to determine the film's form: an unsteady yet vigorous pace, unflinching close-ups of characters' faces, producing claustrophobia but conveying the most recondite emotions. Cassavetes merged fiction and non-fiction, as the duration of the film followed the rhythms of daily life, with the cumulative effect of fusing film-time with lived-time. *Faces* answered, in other words, *Cahiers*' call for film to shatter the idealized or realist mirror of the world by offering a work that was both art and a sharp reflection on contemporary American life.

Cinephiles '68

The special issue on French cinema that *Cahiers* had published in 1965 had already signalled the journal's opposition to policies such as the *avance sur recettes* handed out by the Centre National de la Cinématographie. The ventures were closely linked to President de Gaulle's wider nationalist agenda to safeguard France's culture

76 *Cahiers* 204, September 1968.

at a time when its empire was disintegrating. Editors started to look more closely at distribution structures, working conditions and the role played by the state. Having set down their aim of fighting on the ground, and supporting new cinema, the journal launched a '*Cahiers* week' to counter the CNC's stranglehold on distribution. This was held in two Parisian cinemas, attracting audiences of 10,000, and a programme including new films by Bertolucci, Bellocchio, Skolimowski, Straub and Huillet. It was followed by similar '*Cahiers* days' in Grenoble, Lyon and Marseilles. The *Cahiers* week returned in 1967 with Pasolini and Rocha, and 1968, screening the latest works by Philippe Garrel, Moullet and Herzog. The initiatives resulted in a number of the films being taken into wider distribution in France. This period of cultural activism marked a political and cinematic rapprochement between *Cahiers* and *Positif*, a 'peace in the darkness of the Cinémathèque'.[77] When *Positif* launched its own 'week' in 1968, *Cahiers* encouraged its readers to go along, feeling their programmes would complement each other.

On the eve of May '68, the CNC's attempt to sack the veteran director of the Cinémathèque, Henri Langlois, in a bid to seize control of this juridically independent organization, provoked large, angry demonstrations in Paris that—successfully—demanded his reinstatement. The aura that still surrounds the Affair is partly a result of Langlois's status as a cultural celebrity; already by the sixties he was a living myth. Successive governments had consistently taken a blinkered and lazy approach to the preservation of film stocks. Without Langlois's vision, single-minded commitment and sheer hard work, countless films would have been lost and the young Turks, among many others, would have been deprived of an integral part of their cinematic education. Langlois's sacking was the latest action in an always fraught relationship between the state and the Cinémathèque. A number of attempts had been made to emasculate or dethrone Langlois before 1968.[78]

77 *Cahiers* 184, November 1966.

78 There were, however, long-standing doubts about Langlois's rigour as an archivist: a fire had destroyed some film stock in 1959 and Langlois had wasted an early opportunity to create a modern storage facility for films

Swept up in the revolutionary euphoria of the much broader May events, with factory closures and mass protests, *Cahiers* editors played a leading role in the short-lived 'Estates General of French Cinema' established on 17 May 1968, which proposed the abolition of the CNC and brought together 5,000 students and industry professionals to discuss the complete overhaul of national mechanisms of distribution, regulation and finance.[79] The year's film festivals were also interrupted; the Croisette went completely quiet when Cannes was cancelled, and in Venice four months later many critics and the Estates General—though not *Cahiers* editors—boycotted a round-table discussion on cinema and politics in the heightened political atmosphere.

In terms of concrete changes, however, the mobilization of 1968 yielded nothing for cinema. The Société des Réalisateurs de Films, set up in June to work with the CNC, was really the defeat of the Estates General's earlier demand for its abolition: in 1970, the Estates General itself was dissolved. Not a single reform was passed in the industry, and there was even further hardening of the division between director and technician.

Social and political upheaval had not succeeded, but after 1968, as Serge Daney later recalled, 'no one could make or write about [film] in the same way'. Few directors had immediately documented the period, or offered a cinematic perspective on

---

when the fort at Bois d'Arcy was converted. A second fire in 1980 destroyed Langlois's archivist credibility altogether. In his meticulous reconstruction of the affair, Mannoni explains that the apparently disgraceful role played by Malraux has been distorted: the two men shared a high degree of mutual trust up to 1968, and Malraux's hand had been forced by a third party: the finance minister, who was also buffeted by the growing disgruntlement towards Langlois from outside critics. Mannoni, *L'Histoire de la Cinémathèque Française*.

79 Not all were politicized by the Affair. Langlois himself categorically never crossed the divide between cinema and politics and Truffaut too kept his distance. He rejected Vanessa Redgrave's call for him to attend '68 demonstrations in London, for example, when he discovered these would be in support of Vietnam, not Langlois. Mannoni, *L'Histoire de la Cinémathèque Française*, p. 407.

and interpretation of events. The only filming activity that had taken place simultaneously had been the *cinétracts*—anonymous shorts, coordinated by the Estates General and screened almost immediately in independent venues. These collective works, including contributions from Godard, produced 70,000 metres of film in two months, and some of the material was subsequently reused in features, including Jacques Willemont's *La Reprise du travail aux usines Wonder*.

What critics actually retained from the *cinétracts* experiments were its methods of practice and spirit. In these short works it was possible to assess how cinema might respond in such circumstances, what moving images were able to convey, and the particular role film-makers should play both as creators and as producers.

Collective projects were already a popular form prior to '68 and this activity intensified immediately following the events of that year.[80] Exploiting the *cinéma vérité* techniques and cheaper, more mobile technology, between 1967 and 1977 Chris Marker was part of the Société pour le Lancement des Œuvres Nouvelles (SLON) and its later incarnation, ISKRA, or Images, Son, Kinéscope, Réalisation Audiovisuelle; Godard and Jean-Pierre Gorin's Dziga-Vertov Collective lasted three years from 1968 to 1972. All of these ventures produced a number of militant films, documentaries and commentaries on political events as they unfolded around the world,

80 Collective films were an established and popular genre, especially in France and Italy throughout the sixties. Recent projects included *Ro.Go.Pa.G.* (1962) and *Six in Paris* (1965), but both had been promoted heavily as *auteur* productions. The title of the Italian film was derived from its contributors: Rossellini, Godard, Pasolini. In retrospect, Barbet Schroeder's venture, *Six in Paris* was both swansong and manifesto for the New Wave, 'its end point and its most complete expression' as Douchet has put it. The film also represented the complexity of the split between Rohmer and Rivette at *Cahiers*. Schroeder set the project in motion shortly after the putsch and invited Rohmer, Douchet, Chabrol, Godard, Rouch and Moullet to contribute, but not Rivette or Truffaut. *Loin du Vietnam* (1967) was closer to the collective films that would follow '68, sharing similar political sympathies, filming techniques and preserving the anonymity of each contributor.

from America's war in Vietnam to the Palestinian struggle for liberation and Allende's coup in Chile.

Enemy called Z

At the end of the decade, Costa-Gavras's *Z* provoked much debate in both the mainstream and the cinephile press. It inaugurated what would become—under the Greek director, as well as in the hands of Yves Boisset or André Cayatte and, in its most stylized and intelligent form, of Jean-Pierre Melville—an established genre: the political thriller. These films were an offshoot of the long-running *polar*, a term combining *roman* (novel) and *policier* (detective) that is now an established genre in film and literature, but distinctively French in the ways American cultural models of *noir*, detective fiction and gangsterism are naturalized; narrative and visual conventions were adopted in order to examine real political and social scandals.

Z was one of the biggest cinema hits of sixties France: by the end of 1969, 700,000 people had seen the film in Paris. It recounted the murder in 1963 of politician Gregoris Lambrakis, four years before Greece's democratic government was overthrown by the military. Yves Montand and scriptwriter Jorge Semprún added to the film's left-wing credentials. In *L'Express*, Claude Mauriac named *Z* the must-see film for 'anyone who loves freedom and justice'; *La Croix* emphatically declared it the film that allows you to live, through cinema: 'it will teach you about the world and all of its difficult realities'.[81]

Cahiers and *Positif* were the only publications to disagree with this broad consensus, and Jean Narboni's critique in *Cahiers* in March 1969 was the start of a battle against what became known as the *Série-Z* phenomenon, which would continue into the next decade. Attacking *Z*, Narboni described the film as offering a brand of sterilized militancy in which palpable orderly dissent was realigned with legislative procedures—interviews and interrogations by the police and investigative reporters, and in the law courts—and repackaged for

81 *Téléciné*, vol. 151, no. 2, March–April 1969.

thrills. *Cahiers* immediately shredded the film's political credentials. Narboni argued that its petty-bourgeois ideology was at work 'in the functioning of the film as much as its consumption', because *Z* neglects 'the concrete analysis of concrete situations, the objective study of social relations, the breakdown of political mechanisms'.[82] It was not here, as others had claimed, that you would explore the themes of glory or the decline of democracy; all Costa-Gavras offered was an amiable hero in the form of a kindly, middle-aged doctor confronting angry, faceless hordes on the right-wing outer fringe. There were no real political or moral decisions to be taken, given that characters were so lightly drawn and heavily stereotyped. *Cahiers* challenged the widespread popularity of *Z* because it marked an ominous shift in attitudes post-'68: spectators appeared to be seeking out a cinema that offered the piquancy of politics but that did not implicate or challenge their world view directly. With *Z* you had a film-maker who was addressing politics on the surface, but simultaneously banalizing it. Costa-Gavras was thus perfectly attuned to the changes in public demand: he offered a film that was shot with panache, a lively score, a hint of experimentation (and a lot of those unjustified close-ups again); it was intelligent and committed but never revolutionary, in either narrative content or aesthetic form. This mixture found a receptive audience at the end of the decade.[83]

Lessons from the East

Whilst Costa-Gavras was emerging as the focus of repudiation at *Cahiers*, the journal was also looking backwards to draw instruction from earlier pioneers who could offer insight, as editors sought to develop their theoretical tools and critical tenets. Russian avant-garde from the twenties was especially pertinent, and Direct Cinema was drawing on it via the experimentation with fiction and documentary. Between April 1969 and February 1971 *Cahiers* ran an Eisenstein

82 *Cahiers* 210, March 1969.

83 Alison Smith, *French Cinema in the 1970s: The Echoes of May*, Manchester 2005, pp. 45–6.

series, largely under the direction of Bernard Eisenschitz. Fifteen instalments of Eisenstein's writings were translated and published, and a monograph on the Russian director appeared in May–June 1970. One concept about which Eisenstein had much to teach the *Cahiers* team was montage, hitherto set aside by Bazin in favour of the techniques of deep focus and sequence shots. Dziga Vertov had had some early advocates—Jean Rouch had already taken up the notion of the 'Kino-Eye' in the fifties—and Godard was currently involved in a collective bearing Vertov's name. By the late seventies French semiologist Christian Metz's application of structural linguistics to film was also becoming influential, showing how montage could be employed as a radical concept of film language with an obvious kinship to grammar.

Cahiers published the transcripts of a session at the Aix-en-Provence festival in 1969 devoted entirely to montage; in the same year Rivette, Narboni and Pierre printed their own exploratory discussion around the concept in *Cahiers*. This appeared in experimental form: in four columns, with the main text of the discussion in the two centre blocks and the important endnotes flanking them. It was an attempt to create the effect of montage on the page. Narboni argued that as the technique was an explicit act of manipulation, it could bring the spectator closer to the truth of the film, and make him or her more actively involved in it. Previously montage had been perceived as authoritarian, a technique that imposed a series of univocal and unquestionable meanings on the spectator. Deep focus or the sequence shot retained the 'ambiguity of reality' and the freedom of the spectator, whose eye and interpretation was not subjected to a strictly programmed course. Moving away from this, editors brought Metz's theories into the discussion, citing favourably his formulation of film as a system whereby meaning is produced by difference. Eisenstein's work was understood as a process of linking the elements of a film through the dynamic signs of correlation and integration, bringing them together in such a way that new concepts could emerge.[84]

84 The discussion somewhat caricatured Bazin as anti-montage. Bazin had built his theory of realism as an answer to expressionism—Eisenstein was not his

Manifesto for the next decade

The montage debate marked the beginning of a new and intense period of intellectual inquiry at *Cahiers*. New national cinemas and the revolutionary spirit of '68 acted as the main catalysts, initiating an energetic search for more relevant frameworks for criticism to operate through. This led, above all, to Louis Althusser—though most of the editors engaged with his work *à la sauvage*, having little prior academic formation.[85] The influence of Althusser's thought, in particular his analysis of state apparatuses that disseminate the dominant ideology, quickly made its mark: in October 1969 Comolli and Narboni published an editorial under the title 'Cinema/Ideology/Criticism', which lucidly set out the journal's orientation and interests. The editors explained that their task of 'scientific criticism' must primarily define its field and methods. This necessitated an 'awareness of its own historical and social situation, a rigorous analysis of the proposed field of study, the conditions which make the work necessary and those which make it possible, and the special function it intends to fulfil.'

The editors thus outlined the environment in which *Cahiers* operated—a magazine situated firmly, inevitably, in the economic system of capitalist publishing. They were not, they stressed, utopians: they could not set up a journal that operated independently of this system. *Cahiers* could nonetheless work against it through taking a specific position vis-à-vis films, and consistently and rigorously exposing those that served to transmit the dominant ideology. Under analysis, the function of these films became crystal clear: critics must intervene to make the dominant ideology visible by revealing the film's mechanisms.

Carefully and concisely, Comolli and Narboni discerned seven categories into which all films could be classified. The first and largest, whether 'commercial' or 'art-house', 'modern' or 'traditional', was

---

bête noire. Bazin was also of prime importance to Metz's own theories. See Lee Russell, 'Cinema—Code and Image', *New Left Review* 1/49, May–June 1968.

85 Daney, *La Maison cinéma et le monde 1. Le Temps des Cahiers*, Paris 2001, p. 18.

of films 'imbued through and through with the dominant ideology', and that gave no indication that their makers were even aware of the fact. In form, they 'totally accept the established system of depicting reality: "bourgeois realism" . . . Nothing in these films jars against the ideology'. Offenders on the list included Lelouch, Gérard Oury and Melville. The second category—Straub's *Not Reconciled* and Rocha's *Terra em Transe* were cited—directly challenged the ideological system through both form and subject matter; those in category three did so indirectly (Bergman's *Persona*). Making up the fourth, with Costa-Gavras singled out for criticism, were ostensibly political films that were in fact unremittingly ideological.

The fifth category contained apparently ideological films which actually reveal the ideology to be cracking under its internal tensions. Works by Dreyer and Rossellini were placed here, alongside a number of films by Hollywood directors—works completely integrated into the system but which 'partially dismantled it from within'. The important issue when analysing these films was finding out what made it possible for a film-maker to 'corrode the ideology by restating it in the terms of his film'. The editors believed that the director still remained the most important player here: if he conceives and realizes his film on the deeper level of imagery, not just as a simple celebration of capitalism at the level of story, 'there is a chance it will turn out to be more disruptive'. It would not impact on the ideology itself, but at least break the reflection of it in the film. In the final two categories were 'good' (formally reflective) and 'bad' (pseudo-realist) forms of grass-roots direct cinema.[86]

This was the blueprint for practice that editors took into the seventies. The overarching question had changed—from the Bazinian 'what is cinema?' to 'what is a film today?' How is it produced, manufactured, distributed, understood? It was impossible to answer Bazin's original question 'until a body of knowledge, of theory, has been evolved, to inform at present an empty term, with a concept'. This was the new project. After the glory of its early successes, these veterans of the Rivette putsch were facing the consequences of stripping away

86 *Cahiers* 216, October 1969.

all the early principles and positions set out in the yellow years—foundations that had proved insubstantial when engaging with new national cinemas and the post-'68 landscape. This rejection of classic cinephilia happened in tandem with the editors' politicization. The resulting struggle between accommodating a passion for film and an engagement with politics within one magazine would consume the critical approach of *Cahiers* throughout the seventies.

Rainer Werner Fassbinder, *Gods of the Plague* (1969)

5

1969–1973
Red Notebooks

Daniel Filipacchi had owned *Cahiers* since 1964. The publisher had made few editorial demands during that time. But as the journal's line hardened against everything the millionaire publisher stood for, his position at *Cahiers* became increasingly untenable. When he opened number 216 he found the Althusserian editorial by Comolli and Narboni announcing their determination to fight the capitalist structures which *Cahiers* was subject to—in other words, Filipacchi himself. Turning the page he was met by Raymond Bellour's shot-by-shot breakdown of Tippi Hedren's eventful boat ride in *The Birds*. The package was too much: direct attack from editors, a cinematic masterpiece chopped up and coded, its suspense communicated to readers in the following prose: 'she goes from shots 15–31 (A1: the approach to the dinghy driven by Melanie to the pier by Brenner's house; A2: Melanie's move towards the house), to the return of shots 37–56'. When the following issue showed no softening of its line—an editorial promised that the journal would, under no circumstances, compromise its objectives—Filipacchi put *Cahiers* up for sale.

The disintegration of relations with the publisher led to a collective solution between editors and fellow-travellers, initiated by Truffaut and Doniol-Valcroze. The old guard contributed the majority of funds necessary to buy the journal; current editors and friends put up the rest. In March 1970 a newly independent *Cahiers* re-emerged. The effort to save the journal had brought together the founding generation as well as current editors, but it was the final joint venture of its kind. The opening editorial in the first autonomous issue made no attempt to include discrepant approaches or outlooks. Comolli and Narboni were unequivocal: *Cahiers*' focus must remain steadily on theoretical elaboration, founded on the 'Marxist science of historical materialism and the principles of dialectical materialism'. Relations with the first *Cahiers* generation quickly broke down: as early as October 1970 Truffaut had his name removed from the masthead. The following month *Cahiers* published extracts from statements he had made to another publication, *La Vie Lyonnaise*, explaining the reasons for his departure:

> It is not a disagreement. It is simply that my name in the journal no longer stood for anything. It was quite different in the days when I worked at *Cahiers*. We discussed films in purely aesthetic terms. Nowadays, *Cahiers* has become quite openly political. Editors produce Marxist–Leninist interpretations of films. Nobody except academics can read the journal. As for me, I've never read a line by Marx. But they are doing good work, and they put together substantial reports. Their publication of Eisenstein's writings is excellent.[87]

The relationship between *Cahiers* and Truffaut remained frozen for a decade. The work of Chabrol also came in for some strong criticism. At the start of the seventies he was dismissed as representing the impasse of the New Wave and his *The Breach* treated curtly in a mocking review by Narboni. Chabrol's seventies efforts were poor, and even Truffaut agreed that it was tough but fair, 'at the end of the day, *Cahiers* has not said anything untrue about his work'.[88] One who escaped this 'regime of the "Scottish shower"', as Truffaut put it, was Rohmer. The journal has never turned away from his work, in striking contrast to the fate of the director as editor at the journal. In April 1970, with *Cahiers*' militancy at its peak, Rohmer was invited for interview. The tone announcing the discussion was almost apologetic as editors admitted that everything should oppose them to Rohmer's

87 *Cahiers* 225, November–December 1970.
88 *Cahiers* 225, November–December 1970.

work 'and yet still he interests us, against what he says . . . he has not finished de-routing our route.'[89]

The absolute break with the past was effectively confirmed in October 1972 when the editorial committee of Doniol-Valcroze, Kast and Rivette was removed from the masthead. By 1973 the journal would be almost unrecognizable, transformed into an austere, thick booklet with no photographs and making scant reference to film, instead mapping out the urgent strategies to be undertaken on the 'cultural front'. The issue published at the end of 1973 lacked even a date. This phantom issue epitomized both resurrection and nadir: in three years *Cahiers* had moved from triumphantly regaining its financial independence to completely retreating from the world of contemporary cinema. Editors now operated in an arena of cultural struggle which they had partly fabricated, espousing Marxist–Leninist slogans at every turn. Approximately 11,000 readers had been lost since 1969.[90] This extreme trajectory is only explicable in the context of French political culture at the time, the post '68 energies translating on the left into splinter groups disillusioned with the Communist Party and turning to alternative models: China briefly flashing like a beacon for the dashed revolutionary hopes at home.

Communist persuasions

Cahiers' politicization had occurred on the hoof, the product of clashes with state censorship over Rivette's *La Religieuse* and a few months on the streets protesting on behalf of Henri Langlois. In 1970, consistent with the new Althusserian line, the journal's ties were closest to the PCF—'it appeared to us as the only force [with] a coherent strategy in opposition to the bourgeoisie',[91] but *Cahiers*' grasp of the implications of this allegiance was tenuous. In one of their first major collective texts, editors endorsed without question the Party's political history via their analysis of the collective film

89 *Cahiers* 219, April 1970.
90 Baecque II, pp. 224–6.
91 *Cahiers* 234–5, December 1971/January–February 1972.

made during the Popular Front, *La Vie est à nous*. It was hailed as an exemplary piece of militant cinema, a masterly combination of left-wing politics and revolutionary aesthetics. Renoir as its coordinator had exploited various cinematic genres—a documentary sequence describing the riches of France; fictionalized scenes involving workers, petty bourgeois and small farmers; the in-studio filming of a politician's speech—which exemplified the underlying ideology. *La Vie est à nous* offered a model for revolutionary film-making in technique and effect: the deconstruction of the documentary through a combination of acted and non-acted scenes forced spectators to question the bourgeois outlook on the world.

Deep theory

The early seventies at *Cahiers* were predominantly characterized by the editors' dedication to exploring theoretical models for the analysis of film. This was often done through collective texts: the form befitting a team questioning hierarchical structures and the role of the single author in the production of meaning. In two such texts at the start of the decade, the programme set out in the October 1969 editorial was used to analyse two films from category five—apparently ideological films that reveal the ideology to be cracking under its internal tensions: John Ford's *Young Mr Lincoln* ('the ethical-political face of the capitalist and theological field of Hollywood cinema'), and Josef Sternberg's *Morocco* ('its erotic face'). The ambitious tasks the 1969 editorial had set out made texts distinctly longer than the average article in *Cahiers* up to this point. Both pieces on *Lincoln* and *Morocco* reached 6,000 words. Japanese cinema also received special attention, though the approach was rather suffocating in its abstraction:

> our project is to identify and examine (1) a conception of the subject as 'decentred' and 'diluted' . . . (2) a conception of figuration as a discrete form of coding and not as representation by analogy [and] (3) an explicit articulation of the symbolic domain.[92]

92 Editorial, *Cahiers* 224, October 1970.

It was at this time that *Cahiers*' international influence grew stronger than ever. In Britain, *Screen* had been established as the virtual mirror of its French counterpart in both content and appearance. Editors followed *Cahiers* avidly, and translated many of its texts, including Jean-Pierre Oudart's articles on suture and the collective deconstruction of *Young Mr Lincoln*—now one of *Cahiers*' best-known pieces, included in film studies syllabuses around the world. Oudart's two-part series, published in *Cahiers* in April and May 1969, had introduced psychoanalysis into film studies. Oudart, in Lacanian mode, analysed cinema's attempt to create, by way of suture, an 'illusion of the visible' onto which the spectator projects the phantom of the Absent One. 'The revelation of this absence is the key moment in the fate of the image, since it introduces the image into the order of the signifier, and . . . cinema into the order of discourse'. Traditionally, the counter-shot eradicated this moment of terror and transformed it into a moment of elation.[93] Through these foundational texts, Comolli and Narboni were commended by other editors for their attempts to develop 'a politics, not a poetics, of representation', as the journal contributed to the development of a structuralist theory of cinema around the world.[94]

The main motivation driving *Cahiers*' theoretical texts was to build a materialist model of film, to treat cinema as an object that could and should be broken down into its constituent parts and analysed rigorously. This meant looking closely at montage, discontinuity, the effect of the real and the position of the spectator. Establishing some historical grounding was integral for building such a model—critics needed a heritage to draw from, in the way the yellow years had looked to Hollywood, Renoir, Murnau and Lang. In the early seventies, this came from Russian avant-garde cinema. Truffaut was right that the scholarship involved in producing the Eisenstein series was exemplary. A detailed historical overview was published, and

93 *Cahiers* 211 and 212, April and May 1969.
94 Nick Browne, ed., *Cahiers du cinéma, Volume III, 1969–1972, The Politics of Representation*, London 1990, p. 12.

texts by Lev Kuleshov, Anatoly Lunacharsky, Yuri Tynianov and Dziga Vertov were all translated. For *Cahiers* these figures represented 'our immediate past' and 'our present'. As the 1969 editorial had made clear:

> The only possible line of advance seems to be to use the theoretical writing of the Russian film-makers of the twenties (Eisenstein above all), to elaborate and apply a critical theory of cinema, a specific method of apprehending rigorously defined objects, in direct reference to the method of dialectical materialism.

The Soviet avant-garde provided *Cahiers* with a framework to develop its own nascent theories around what constituted 'ideological victory in the area of form', as Eisenstein had described his own *Strike*. The earlier discussions around montage had been tentative steps in this direction, as had the collective text on *La Vie est à nous*, but the highly developed tradition from the Russians offered more in both theory and practice.

Significantly, in their engagement with this work, *Cahiers* connected aesthetics directly with political engagement. Formal analysis was combined with cultural struggle on the ground as revolutionary potential was derived from artistic technique, which could eventually lead to broader social change. The struggle on the cultural front should thus take a primary role in the activity of any critic—it was a vital arena for provoking and promoting the class struggle itself.

Farewell, silver screen

The start of the seventies at *Cahiers* involved, in fact, very rich critical work. Close attention was paid to a wide variety of films from around the world, subject either to hard criticism or ebullient praise. The œuvres of Jancsó, Nagisa Oshima and the Taviani brothers were celebrated; films singled-out for discussion were Buñuel's *Tristana*, Fellini's *Clowns*, Robert Kramer's *Ice*, Straub and Huillet's *Othon* and Tati's *Traffic*. The archives were explored not only for the Russian masters but also for early American pioneers: in a remarkable series spanning four issues, D. W. Griffith's *Intolerance*, the silent epic from

1916, was rerun on paper, with a text-only, shot-by-shot description. Every issue featured a detailed critical round-up of the new films being made from around the world.

However, this productivity reduced the more *Cahiers* editors became concerned with issues of politics *tout court*. The world releases section was suppressed at the end of 1971, along with most current film material. The magazine's reputation and influence may have been growing abroad, but at home the situation was darkening. In the aftermath of 1968, state repression of far-left militants was stepped up, particularly in the factories. The Maoist Gauche Prolétarienne group was banned in 1970, and within two years over a thousand activists had been sentenced to prison. While Althusser's PCF, in negotiations with the Socialists over a common programme for a united left, distanced itself from what was going on, other left intellectuals—Sartre, de Beauvoir, Foucault, and even the scarcely political Truffaut—rallied to the Maoists' defence, distributing the GP paper, *La Cause du peuple*, on the streets. Althusser's personal openness to the Cultural Revolution had permitted a common intellectual front between his followers and *maoisant* elements; now, however, this front came under increasing pressure.

Thus as *Cahiers*' programme became more politicized, the coverage of film and especially targets for attack were increasingly rare. Only the *Série-Z* 'political thrillers' remained targets. Comolli and Pascal Bonitzer, a critic since the sixties, were provoked to set out a clearer line between film and politics by two apparently political films: Karmitz's *Camarades* and Costa-Gavras's *L'Aveu*. Taking *Camarades* to task, Bonitzer rejected the film on the grounds that no work could avoid bending to the dominant ideology when made with the conscious aim of attracting a large audience, which Karmitz's had been. In more programmatic mode, Comolli outlined fifteen propositions for what made a film political, with starting points for constructing a proper theory for their analysis. Costa-Gavras's work was an aberration of all the elements that made an authentic work in this model. His films created the illusion of a political discourse through the fiction when really they fell at the first hurdle, not doing the 'preliminary work politically necessary to all political discourse: a questioning of the work's conditions of existence and its means'. Straub and Huillet's *Othon* was the counter-example used by Comolli. *Othon* was cinema in which politics existed in and through the very material composition of the work, rather than superficially in the screenplay.[95]

In 1971 the atmosphere in France, and among groups on the left especially, was highly charged. A new *guerre de papier* was sparked by the anti-Althusserian *Positif* editorial 'Les enfants du paradigme', leading *Cahiers* into a brief alliance with the literary journal *Tel Quel* and the newly-founded *Cinéthique*. Robert Benayoun, one of *Positif*'s editors, had attacked all three when he praised the work of Christian Metz but denounced his disciples for their pretentious and obscure texts. Metz replied in defence of his colleagues at *Cinéthique*, *Cahiers* and *Tel quel*, and the three journals published a joint response in January 1971, charging this 'anti-theoretical left' with political opportunism, 'masking' and 'distorting' the development of Marxist–Leninist theoretical work and 'censorship' of its scientific base, namely historical and dialectical materialism, in 'radical opposition to idealism in all areas of social practice'. *Cahiers* announced with *Cinéthique* and *Tel quel* that 'the recognition of the antagonistic contradiction between the bourgeoisie and the proletariat' should 'serve as the starting point for considering all the contradictions that mobilize social processes in France today'.[96] Comolli's six-part series on 'Technology and Ideology', started in May 1971, paved the way for a more specifically Maoist view of culture in *Cahiers*. He refuted the conceptualization of culture found in Bazin, Jean Mitry and the French Communist Party, arguing instead that film technology could only be understood as culturally determined, and developing as a result of ideology.

Why Maoism?

From its non-official allegiance to the PCF, to dedicated Marxist–Leninism by the end of 1971, *Cahiers*' itinerary should be understood as a direct reflection of the broader cultural and

95 *Cahiers* 222 and 224, July and October 1970.
96 *Cahiers* 226–227, January–February 1971.

intellectual trends of the day, as well as resulting from the strong influence of a few figures over the journal at this time. *Tel quel*, briefly significant for *Cahiers*, had broken with the PCF and embraced Maoism in 1971; more importantly, Godard had been close to the Gauche Prolétarienne for a time.[97] In fact, seeking a re-connection with Godard since his withdrawal into collective film-making in the late sixties is key to explaining *Cahiers*' red turn. The rationale behind the rapprochement with *Cinéthique* lies here: Godard, ignoring *Cahiers*, had been in touch with *Cinéthique* shortly after it was founded in 1969. Its focus was the analysis of the relationship between aesthetics and ethics in film analysis. *Cinéthique* was overtly left wing and did not share *Cahiers*' continued interest in clarifying the contradictions characteristic of mainstream cinema, pursuing instead the experimental and avant-garde. *Cinéthique* editors, to Godard's approval, were more active on the distribution and exhibition circuit, seeking out alternative channels and dedicated to advancing what it designated as 'materialist' cinema.[98] The first suggestion of a Maoist inclination came in October 1971, with the publication of *Cahiers*' declaration at the Porretta–Terma festival. In it, editors explicitly referred to the Chinese Cultural Revolution, and stated that they were 'sick of being the hard-line in a soft party'. Their Marxist–Leninist allegiance was made official in the end-of-year editorial. Here, editors engaged in a full-blown auto-critique of their previous positions:

97 The Maoist GP was set up in 1968 and officially disbanded in 1973. Its leading figure was Benny Lévy, but other members included; André Glucksmann; Serge July, founder of *Libération*; Jacques-Alain Miller; Jean-Claude Milner; and Olivier Rolin. See Michael Scott Christofferson, *French Intellectuals Against the Left. The Anti-Totalitarian Moment of the 1970s*, New York and Oxford 2004, pp. 57–64.

98 *Cinéthique*'s interests prefigured some of *Cahiers*', though the two were initially in dispute over whether or not a revolutionary technique in film could produce scientific knowledge, or, as *Cahiers* asserted in November 1969, cinema was an ideological product and could only serve different ideologies. Sylvia Harvey, *May 68 and Film Culture*, London 1980.

> We repressed the cultural contradiction in the name of support for the avant-garde faction of the PCF, and we repressed the political contradiction by refusing to recognize a fundamental incompatibility between our passive approval of the Party's politics and our consideration of the Chinese position.[99]

The auto-critique looked back over the years 1969 to 1971, directing especially disparaging comments towards the text on *La Vie est à nous*. Editors deprecated their 'word-for-word and uncritical' acceptance of the film's theses, which offered a faithful rendition of the French Communist Party's account of the Popular Front period. Now, PCF revisionism was identified as the great enemy against which editors must rally.

What *Cahiers* proposed in taking up the Marxist–Leninist line was to develop its own domestic variant of a 'Revolutionary Cultural Front' by which a new revolutionary party would develop, forging closer links with the French working class. In July 1972 a *Cahiers* seminar at the Avignon festival issued a manifesto of tasks to be achieved on this cultural front. For over a year, much of *Cahiers*' contents was given over to the means of enacting these through careful studies of the forms of popular culture and how best to master cultural animation. Texts were provided by activists including the Maoist Lou Sin group, formed by Censier University students.

The main instigator of this 'Front Q' was Philippe Pakradouni, who had followed Narboni's classes at Vicennes. He entered *Cahiers* in September 1972 and saw in the journal 'a red base to take the offensive to the masses' and a 'tool of ideological cultural struggle'.[100] It was a moment when *Cahiers* was vacillating over which direction it should take, with editors scratching their heads over what exactly 'a magazine with the name *Cahiers du cinéma* should do' in the present climate.[101] The Pakradouni effect was immediate: editors were duly dispatched around the country to screen militant films and animate discussions; the journal's reports of these initiatives left scarcely any room for the

99 *Cahiers* 234–235, December 1971–February 1972.

100 *Cahiers* 242–243, November 1972.

101 Editorial discussion on 29 September 1972, quoted in Baecque II, p. 257.

critical analysis of film. The struggle, as it was now perceived, did not require a theory of cinema's specificity. It needed troops on the frontline—usually intellectuals pulled from their desks—to take film to the people, and have people make their own films.

Departures, expulsions, resignations and new arrivals characterized these red years: PCF member Bernard Eisenschitz was subject to a mock trial in light of his frequent contributions to the communist journal *Nouvelle Critique*, and promptly drummed out; the long-standing and illustrious editorial board disappeared, and Sylvie Pierre quit in 1973 in disagreement over the Maoist turn. Pakroudini had the field to himself, along with another recent recruit, Serge Toubiana (b. 1949), a *grenoblois* Lou Sin militant studying at Censier where Bonitzer, Daney and others were teaching film. Godard returned to the fold when he worked with the editors to compile a history of the Dziga-Vertov group published in the May–June 1972 issue, which also ran the full dialogue from the collective's film, 'Luttes en Italie', and a comparative essay on Karmitz's *Blow for Blow* and *Tout va bien*, Godard and Jean-Pierre Gorin's new film on workers' revolts, post-1968.

The sales of the journal were only going down, however. Production costs had to be cut as the number of readers plummeted from 14,000 issues bought in 1969 to 3,000 in 1973 (subscribers and universities generally remained faithful; the big drop was in off-the-shelf sales). The design was radically changed in November 1972. Its rebarbative sobriety was an economic necessity, but also reflected the essentially anti-cinema stance, providing one response to Godard's troubling question: 'How does one represent capitalist exploitation?' Publication was at its most erratic in these years—seven issues were released in 1970 and 1971, five in 1972 and 1973, four in 1974.

The Maoist movement was effectively over in France even before *Cahiers* joined it. And yet the editors were completely engrossed in the close planning of their Revolutionary Cultural Front to be launched at the 1973 Avignon festival. When the moment finally came, it was a disaster: four days of sectarian squabbling and a miserable turnout. 'The artists were intimidated, inhibited by the weight of errors to be avoided and tasks to be undertaken, while the militants hid their lack of ideas behind generalizations', Daney would later recall. The reality of the Front Q had been to bring together 'people like us, who wanted to politicize culture', with *groupuscules* of former far-left militants, knowing they had been defeated politically but now seeking a second front where they could 'carry on intimidating people while negotiating their survival'. The most adept, such as André Glucksmann, re-invented themselves within a few short years as Reaganite liberals and *nouveaux philosophes* of anti-totalitarianism.[102]

The denouement of the red years

After Avignon, *Cahiers* editors returned to Paris gloomy and lost. The Front Q had been a dead end. Comolli and Narboni were increasingly detached from the journal, the former working on his own films and the latter busy teaching. Bonitzer and Toubiana moved decisively to oust Pakroudini, who had treated *Cahiers* as a political tool and had no interest whatsoever in cinema. Serge Daney started to lay the foundations for yet another reorientation and redefinition of *Cahiers*' role, in his three-part series 'The Critical Function'—something which had been all but lost in the feverish militant activism. Critics were to address current films before making any political pronouncements, and this attempt to bring the two together led *Cahiers*' programme for the latter half of the seventies.

The scientific clarity of Comolli and Narboni's editorial in 1969 had provided a basis for close analysis without denying that a film was also a work of art, irreducible to its conditions of production.

---

102 Daney, *La Maison 1*, p. 22. Alain Badiou—one who did not change his spots—dismisses many associations with Maoism as a pure modish fad: 'Maoism of the Gauche Prolétarienne type was very marked by having been fashionable among intellectuals for five years or so, say from 1969 to 1974, and many people gravitated to it for that reason—as well as Sollers [editor of *Tel Quel*] and Sartre, there was Godard, for example. What attracted these intellectuals and artists was an aura of activism and radicalism, and they didn't look too closely at the actual politics the GP was conducting, which often invoked trickery and throwing dust in people's eyes. Almost everything put out by GP propaganda was half untrue—where there was a kitten, they described a Bengal tiger.' Interview appears in Eric Hazan, *Changement de propriétaire*, Paris 2007, p. 97; English translation in *New Left Review* 53, 'Roads to Renegacy', September–October 2008.

But the tenet that all films are political was a dead end for critics of cinema. Demanding that only revolutionary techniques can question bourgeois ideology yoked the context and source of a film together with its final result. This hindered engagement with any purportedly bourgeois product and ultimately outlawed the consideration of most contemporary films that the rest of the world was watching.

Cahiers had nothing to say about cinema in 1973, but reams on how a cultural struggle could be invigorated through the use of experimental cinema as catalyst. Directors who believed in freedom from dogmatism, to create the films they saw fit, were entirely ignored. In Germany, Fassbinder—a devotee of *Cahiers'* canon who dedicated his first film to Chabrol, Rohmer and Straub—had already made over ten extraordinary films that drew a portrait of contemporary German society using a mixture of Brecht, Sirk and the New Wave; India's Satyajit Ray had long since completed his Apu Trilogy; a strong body of work was emerging from the Senegalese Ousmane Sembène; Tarkovsky's œuvre was in full genesis; Bergman was entering his late phase, while from the saturated and beautiful *Oedipus Rex* and sober atheism of *The Gospel According to Matthew*, Pasolini's work (and shortly afterwards, his life) would come to an abrupt and shocking end with *Salò*. There was little trace of this in *Cahiers*. Even at home, with the exception of Straub, Huillet, Godard and perhaps Jean Eustache, no-one was reckoned to be of interest; not Maurice Pialat, nor Jean-Pierre Melville (who was unkindly advised to make a career out of trench-coat commercials).[103]

Few worthwhile judgements on films were emitted in the red years. If the principles that drove this period—opposition to the development of mainstream pictures, the impact on avant-garde work—are laudable, less so were the results. It was the time when the journal absorbed French political and social currents most dramatically, reflecting the vacillation of the aesthetic project after the rich and explosive early years. In the sixties these principles

---

103 Serge Daney, quoted in Ginette Vincendeau, *Jean-Pierre Melville: An American in Paris*, London 2003, p. 16.

were scrutinized and new avenues explored. To its credit, *Cahiers* did not reconfigure itself around a single model from another discipline: structuralism, psychoanalysis, linguistics—none proved satisfactory. So, the critic as militant was another potential trajectory. It was a model that depended on the broader social and cultural environment, however, and it had to play itself out to its extreme conclusion before its shortcomings were finally accepted. The question then was whether, when the activism of the red years failed, there were still strong radical intentions and, crucially, enough basic faith in cinema for editors to rebuild anew the *Cahiers* project.

Eric Rohmer, *A Tale of Springtime* (1990)

6

1974–1981
The Daney Years

The seventies was *Cahiers'* most manifold, contradictory and at times radical decade. The first years were red, before the editors' collective and individual failure at Avignon in 1973 brought an end to *Cahiers* as an organ of cultural struggle, and once more threw open the debate over the review's specific position in relation to politics, the art of film, its spectators and creators. When re-engagement began in 1974, there were new players and issues to take into account.

Hollywood had spawned a crop of directors fresh out of film school who called themselves *auteurs* because they had learnt about the term in class, but their work offered little formal or creative originality, nor any specific world view through the *mise en scène*. In other national film industries there was a comparatively lively avant-garde and independent scene, especially in Germany, Latin America and Eastern Europe. Globally, television had established itself as the primary transmitter of images. In France the political climate was turning away from the high radicalism of the late sixties. In its place came a quite different prospect: in 1975 Valéry Giscard d'Estaing was elected president on the promise of a definitive break with Gaullism. The country was on course towards a 'new society' that would embrace liberal values.

Since 1971 *Cahiers* had been concentrating all its energies on bringing the cultural struggle to its readers. When this project failed, the journal lost its driving motivation, its *raison d'être*. Editors had been intent on extinguishing their original, deep and passionate belief in the art of cinema, and replacing it with another: a belief in their role as active shapers of social revolution, through acts of bringing art to the masses. But they now needed to reclaim the critical distance from the world they had abolished.

The chief editors left in 1974 to pursue individual projects, the humiliation of Avignon and a more generalized political pessimism weighing heavily on their shoulders. But before leaving, Comolli and Narboni elected their replacement team, passing the baton to a 'tandem' of Serge Daney and Serge Toubiana. This duo would, they hoped, complement each other. Readership had dipped below 3,000 and production had become totally erratic. It was envisaged that Toubiana, with his strong organizational and management qualities, could get the journal back on track financially. Daney by contrast was the poet and thinker; he would develop *Cahiers*' critical function by fostering a better relationship between political militancy and cinephilia. Their contrasting views of cinema—as an industry, as an ever-changing art—was not yet a problem, as both pulled together to save *Cahiers* from impending shipwreck. Daney and Toubiana had to navigate the journal away from the austere, dogmatic rejection of everything considered cinema that had come to characterize it during the Maoist years.

What's in a name?

The question that came back time and again and provoked many heated arguments was over *Cahiers*' identity as a film journal. What did this mean? Looking back at the history of the magazine, editors saw a number of potential paths already pursued. Between 1969 and 1971 *Cahiers* had produced the articles that had established its reputation and earned it high esteem abroad. Perhaps it should settle for being an academic journal, dedicating itself to advanced theoretical research? Or was its real contribution at the level of film aesthetics? The yellow years with Bazin and the young Turks had produced the original concepts of *mise en scène* and *auteur*; in the sixties there were close explorations of poetic realism and Direct Cinema; preoccupations in the seventies were over the use of sound and off-screen space.

Another model was journalism. Perhaps the style and approach of the 'Petit Journal du Cinéma'—short bulletins at the back of the magazine, in place since 1955—should be expanded? Daney and Toubiana had both been writing reviews for *Libération* since 1973, which had influenced the way they viewed the critic's role, Daney in particular taking much from the experience. He found that the quick turnover and the non-specialist readership he was addressing forced him to ask on a more regular basis, and with a greater sense of urgency, the questions of how to intervene and who to privilege in his analysis. Writing in this format, Daney could envisage more easily an ideological battle that was not taking place in a vacuum. Rather, he felt part of a real struggle with stakes set down clearly against a concrete enemy—'reactionary, fascist films'—and that, when writing and engaging in this fight, journalists had to take into consideration the addressee: the reader.

All these possible models were on the table, and editors experimented with them in the magazine. The increasing turn to the areas of production was emphasized when two theoretical models for understanding film were openly rebuked by Jean-Louis Schefer and Pierre Legendre in their *Cahiers* interviews in 1978. Psychoanalysis and semiology were out, they argued; instead, technicians such as Jean-Pierre Beauviala, a close collaborator with Godard and innovator in photographic and televisual technology, provided greater sources of inspiration.[104] The various possible models provoked yet deeper questions: what remained of the *politique des auteurs*, now that revered directors had disappeared or been knocked off their pedestals by alternative models of creativity? What relationship existed between the early masters and contemporary cinema? What was a modern-day cinephile after the audience had been dragged into the daylight via interrogations over the nature of spectatorship? The once intimate bond between viewers and film had been redefined as

104 Beauviala was first interviewed in February 1978, having met Bergala in Grenoble where he worked with Godard. Beauviala was the technical brain behind Godard's creativity, heading Aäton, a business that developed very portable 16mm and 35mm cameras. A month after his interview he was elected to the board of directors alongside Daney, Narboni and Toubiana, and in 1979 became the journal's scientific advisor.

a suffocating affiliation, or an act of blind faith. How strongly should political convictions direct and influence the critical work of a film journal? What was cinema's 'specificity', given the proliferation of images through advertising and television? And how should the critic conceive of his or her role within this transformed landscape of images?

The tandem in action

As they began to answer some of these questions, Daney and Toubiana did not entirely recant their previous commitments. Their first editorial recognized, however, that *Cahiers* had become a 'cadre school' and 'political bureau', losing sight of its necessary character as a film journal: 'in the interests of abstract politicism, we ran the risk of cutting ourselves off from the constituency of cinema . . . In the end our "right to be heard" was becoming ambiguous'.[105]

Daney proposed a solution, or at least the foundations for one, in 'The Critical Function', the first instalment appearing in that undated issue after Avignon and concluding at the end of 1974. In the series he outlined a model for a criticism that was 'neither a catalogue of what is beautiful (old-style cinephilia) nor an account of what is wrong (new-style dogmatism)', but rather 'something more heterogeneous . . . less settled', in the name of 'something which is not given, which exists in embryo, in the form of scattered elements'. This tentative outline was expressed in the rest of the journal as major interventions, such as 'A Certain Tendency in French Cinema', which engaged with national productions after a long silence. Although the title boldly reprised Truffaut's manifesto of twenty years before, this article was quite literally composed of notes and fragments by Daney, Kané, Oudart and Toubiana.

This restless multifariousness and the uncertainty over *Cahiers*' identity left the magazine open to incoherence. And indeed, *Cahiers* simultaneously engaged with the carnivalesque and a continuing commitment to militant cinema and language-derived theorization. It ran investigations into racism, pornography and the radical *commedia*

105 *Cahiers* 250, June 1974.

dell'arte of Dario Fo. The cinemas of the Maghreb and Sub-Saharan Africa were explored, with some apprehension. Writers on the subject were exclusively 'natives', as though *Cahiers* editors had not the confidence to speak about an 'other' cinema; interviews with Borhan Alaouié from the Middle East, the Mauritian Sidney Sokhna and Algeria's Abdelaziz Tolbi focused on conditions of production and the political struggle without addressing aesthetic and formal qualities. When Toubiana reviewed Miguel Littín's *The Promised Land*, he found the Chilean director's film remarkable for the 'positivity' of the presentation of the protagonist-hero in history, and the nature of the struggle 'exemplary'— descriptive qualities that would have been scrupulously unpicked if attributed to European cinema.[106]

Yet whatever its eclecticism, the *Cahiers* of the mid-seventies still held true to Doniol-Valcroze's summary: 'We are for A, B and C, and against X, Y and Z'. Certain theorists were invited for interview in the search for new critical models, including Gilles Deleuze, Marc Ferro and Jacques Rancière. Deleuze explored Godard's *Number Two*, Ferro was interviewed on the said and the unsaid in film history and propaganda, and Rancière discussed the significance of 1968 and the traces of history and ideology behind documentary and fiction film images. His *La Leçon d'Althusser* had been instrumental in breaking the philosopher's influence on *Cahiers* editors. Toubiana and Daney credited the book with 'helping us to position ourselves outside a frozen and sterile dialectic, where classes, authorities and ideologies just sit and exchange evil looks: this book gave us a better understanding of the game of ideologies, their intertwining system and their opposition.'[107]

None of these thinkers had an overwhelming influence on the review, but all were fellow travellers for a time. Deleuze in particular was a passionate cinephile, and attended *Cahiers* screenings in the mid-seventies.[108] Pascal Bonitzer was taken by his *Anti-Oedipus* (1972) and

---

106 *Cahiers* 253, October–November 1974.

107 *Cahiers* 268–269, July–August 1976.

108 Deleuze first wrote on cinema in 1974, and contributed to *Positif* and *Le Cinématographe*. He taught at Vincennes alongside Jean Narboni, and from his courses developed his two main works on cinema, *The Movement-*

integrated Deleuze's thought into his articles on film aesthetics, finding more in it than in the work of Christian Metz, whose semiological readings had, he confessed, remained too much at a distance and too abstract. In contrast, Deleuze believed in cinema as an artistic creation, and had a 'sharp and personal grasp of the film-makers we loved'.[109]

Murderer as hero

If Deleuze appealed to editors' re-emerging cinephilia, Michel Foucault provided a continued political framework through which to channel it. *Cahiers* held two interviews with Foucault (1974 and 1976), in which he offered a theoretical model to attack a tendency the magazine had scornfully termed 'retro style' in a crop of recent French films. At the time, Foucault was developing his notion of the 'specific intellectual' against the classic and universal Sartrean model. He warned against cultural representations of history that could lead to what he called 'false archaeologizing'. By this he meant the construction of popular memory via pulp literature, compulsory education, cinema and television. For Foucault, the act of false archaeologizing was a characteristic of the twentieth century, and had the effect of recoding the amount of historical knowledge that classes—especially the working class—had about themselves. At *Cahiers* the emplacement of cinema within the generic 'culture' was implicitly accepted, and some films were correspondingly analysed as pure products of it. Louis Malle's *Lacombe Lucien* was one example. Daney demolished the film by arguing that Malle exemplified the 'retro style' by filming a protagonist unaware of his own history, through which events pass without his taking account of them. Thus the film could disavow the fact that the working class played its part in the Resistance.

Image and *The Time-Image*. *Cahiers* interviewed him after each publication, in 1983 and 1985 respectively. His main references in the books were drawn directly from the magazine's canon: Hitchcock, Renoir, Ford, Godard. For Deleuze's particular affinity with Daney's criticism, see the preface he wrote to Daney's *Ciné-journal*, Paris 1986.

109 Quoted in Françoise Dosse, *Gilles Deleuze et Félix Guattari. Biographie croisée*, Paris 2007.

In his second interview, around René Allio's *I, Pierre Rivière, Having Slaughtered My Mother, My Sister and My Brother . . .*, Foucault described the contrasting case of eighteen-year-old Pierre Rivière, who in 1835 murdered his mother, sister and brother. Whilst in prison Rivière had written a meticulous account of his acts, describing the background to the murder and explaining his motivations: to free his father from, as he presented it, a cruel, exploitative wife. Foucault had come across the original text when researching the genesis of institutions such as the prison and the asylum. Under his direction, it was republished in 1975 and Foucault collaborated with René Allio to adapt the text to the screen. Bonitzer and Toubiana were co-writers on the script. For Foucault, Rivière was a man fully conscious of his actions, who had, by writing his text, taken a stand against being forgotten or ignored and simply assimilated by the system as 'mad'. *Cahiers* editors agreed with this portrait. 'The system discovers one who prevents it from functioning', Toubiana argued, celebrating Rivière for 'teaching the law a few things about itself; he prevents the code from codifying, the norm from normalizing, the law from being applied'. To every institution that wanted to explain his act, Rivière resisted, proving they did not have an answer to everything.

The most powerful aspect of Allio's film was its explanation of the murders through the evocation of the life of peasants in France. Rivière witnessed the long and ugly battle between his mother—greedy for money and a life of leisure—and his father, a good but weak man, easily exploited by her at first, later claiming what was 'his' (possessions, land, children). By writing his memoir Rivière had represented the 'peasant class taking language into its own hands'. What enthused *Cahiers* editors in 1976, however, was the specifically Foucauldian twist on this: Rivière was an example of the failure of reason itself—reason being, in Foucault's conception, inherently oppressive and normalizing. Rivière was a boy who had committed a monstrous act in desperate response to a bleak existence. He appears also to have been capable of seeing beyond his own circumstances: autodidact, imaginative, inventive, he had the potential to transform his life. But for Foucault and for *Cahiers*, rather more implausibly, Rivière offered more than the spirit of rebellion and resistance turned sour: he questioned the 'status of knowledge' as it was being institutionalized through education, science and law.

Around Rivière, *Cahiers* editors could express their own ambivalence towards universal and objective truth. For Bonitzer the Rivière case—which had brought to light all the documents related to the case at the time, including doctors' reports, lawyers' statements and press coverage—showed that 'the false is to be found at the heart of journalistic "truth", psychiatric "truth" and the "truth" of the penal law'. *Pierre Rivière* was a *Cahiers* film, and the politics that drove the sympathy for Rivière conveys the extent to which editors subscribed to Foucault's critique of Enlightenment principles, especially under attack post '68 and after the Maoist phase.[110]

The film has survived its politics: it remains a genuinely cinematic consideration of how history might be filmed, how a true story can be conveyed through fictitious tools—script, constructed scenes, costumes—without compromising historical accuracy. Allio had wanted to achieve more than what he judged as the 'flat imitation' style of Pasolini, and his project was closer to traditional realism. Rivière's acts are rooted in their context via a simple *mise en scène*, using non-actors whose sometimes wooden delivery further removed any misleading veneer of fiction. At the same time, we are constantly reminded of the artifice by devices such as panning shots, protagonists' pieces to camera and the freezing of the action into momentary stills. Consequently, the work provides an example of the art surviving the politics that generated it. For *Cahiers* it shows that editors' engagement with cinema rather than straight politics led to more powerful and enduring results.

Who speaks?

The question of 'who speaks' had dominated the discussion and interest around *Pierre Rivière*, and Daney took this up in his articles on the critical function. There were many layers in each film, and Daney drew these out by distinguishing between *énoncé*, or statement, and its *énonciation*, utterance, or cinematic presentation

110 All above citations from *Cahiers* 271, November 1976.

of the statement. These terms were vital for Daney, because they allowed him to orient the critical function towards a consideration of who controls the discourse in a film and how ideas are expressed. 'How can political statements be presented cinematically? How can they be made positive?' Daney asked. He argued that the critic can respond to these questions by distinguishing between the statement and the enunciation:

> criticizing a film does not mean shadowing it with complicit discourse [or] unfolding it or opening it out. It means *opening it up* along this imaginary line which passes between statement and utterance, allowing us to read them side by side, in their problematical, disjointed relationship.[111]

Cahiers had broadly adopted Foucault's formulation of false archaeologizing and took forward his focus on marginalized groups by looking at how they were represented in film. For editors coming to terms with the collapse of their performance as political activists, Foucault's argument that revolutions must—can only—be enacted on a small scale, because institutions were totally ridden with power's tentacular grip, was attractive at the time.

This outlook was in evidence in the 1975 notes on French cinema. Editors were unanimous in their criticism of what they described as the 'new naturalism' displayed in films by Bertrand Blier, Jacques Doillon or Claude Berri. The style was loosely defined as the presentation of a familiar France with no hint of theatricality; directors reflecting little on cinematic technique and instead emphasizing a strong narrative around the marginalized—immigrants, the working class, women, youth—and issues such as poverty and racism. Such directors were echoing wider national concerns around how society might be restructured under plans put forward by the prime minister, Jacques Chaban-Delmas, to raise France to the standards of modern, developed capitalism. In the aftermath of 1968, new social actors had been brought to the fore but had little in the way of organized politics

111 *Cahiers* 250, May 1974.

through which they could channel their energies.[112] For *Cahiers*, the new naturalism was lazily projecting these groups onto the big screen and locating them at the centre of the story as though they had always been there.

> They are 'naturalized' in every sense of the word, recognized by the law, made normal, natural and legal, and accede to a sort of 'iconic dignity'. But what is not registered in this process (the foundation of naturalism and its *raison d'être*) is how and why they *break into* the story.[113]

Godard provided an alternative. He had returned to feature-making with a tongue-and-cheek take on workers' revolution in the aftermath of 1968. *Tout va bien*—already commended by *Cahiers* in 1972—successfully showed the irruption of marginalized groups into society without simultaneously normalizing this process. Godard achieved this by virtue of his specific cinematic presentation, or enunciation. In a supermarket scene, for example, he transformed the space into a social theatre, undermining the realism of the image—brightly lit, monotonous aisles full of obedient bodies robotically filling their shopping carts—by an impossibly long tracking shot showing an endless line of check outs. This destroyed the impression of reality, which validated the rebellion of the hitherto placid consumers who

112 The Jacobinism of French politics provides one explanation for why the new social movements made relatively little impact in France. Another is the simultaneous rise and gathering of momentum of the official Left at the time. Both the Socialists and the PCF were keen to co-opt the energies of various post '68 rebellious currents, forcing the new social movements to choose between independence and integration. The latter promised a degree of political effectiveness at the price of accepting parts of the official Left's politics. The consequence was the division and severe weakening of most of the movements: the 'vacuum cleaner' effect. Those segments that resisted integration (and remained outside the unions) rapidly divided into small competing groups whose conflicts further undercut the movements' position. See George Ross, 'Where Have All the Sartres Gone? The French Intelligentsia Born Again', in James Hollingfield and George Ross, eds, *Searching for the New France*, London 1991, p. 231.

113 Daney, *Cahiers* 257, May–June 1975.

reject the rules of the game, refusing to pay for their goods and charging out of the supermarket, leaping off the conveyer belt of consumerism to storm the checkout barricades.[114]

JMS and JLG

Throughout the later seventies, Godard's film-making was, as always, a constant focal point for defining *Cahiers'* critical foundations. He topped the list of directors the journal was decisively *pro*, even though Godard himself had kept his distance since the Filipacchi era. Relations thawed in 1976 when he met Daney and Toubiana for a series of discussions in Grenoble.[115]

At the other extreme in terms of practice and vision were Jean-Marie Straub and Danièle Huillet. *Cahiers* embraced this pair and Godard as part of the same world; indeed, in their radically different styles, cinema was reinventing itself. Straub and Huillet, who worked frequently in Germany and Italy, had been considered vital *auteurs* at *Cahiers* since Rivette engaged with their work in the sixties. In the Spartan red years the duo were amongst the select few to receive sustained attention throughout, and in 1975 *Cahiers* dedicated its entire summer issue to their filmed production of Schoenberg's opera *Moses and Aaron*. The coverage was the closest analysis of any single film undertaken by *Cahiers* in this period. The long interview with Straub presented a view of cinema that the journal briefly adopted, specifically his refusal to compromise aesthetics, subject matter and

---

114 Godard had already employed the technique of distancing by means of long tracking shots, in his 1967 film *Weekend*. Here city denizens fleeing to the country for a 'relaxing weekend away' get stuck in a traffic jam, but one that goes on, and on. As we see the stationary cars multiply to an impossible number, the antics become increasingly disturbing and the dark side of taking the weekend away is unearthed. Brian Henderson, 'Towards a Non-Bourgeois Camera Style', *Film Quarterly*, vol. 24, no. 2, 1971.

115 The reconciliation was confirmed when Godard and Anne-Marie Miéville—his permanent collaborator since the two had met in 1970; shortly after, she provided the still photographs for *Tout va bien*—accepted the invitation to edit *Cahiers*' 300th issue in May 1979.

cinematic language for the sake of mass appeal. Straub defended instead 'minority' cinema in the hope that those few that saw and received his works today might, 'as Lenin said, be the majorities of tomorrow'.[116]

The specific orientation of *Cahiers* was set out most clearly in Pascal Bonitzer's 1976 article, 'J. M. S. and J. L. G.' Here he outlined the two poles of film-making, and in doing so suggested that *Cahiers* might concentrate on the most experimental and avant-garde works in production, and devote its writing not exclusively but most passionately to those operating outside the industry. Bonitzer sketched out a possible new framework for delineating the boundaries of the seventh art:

> They stand at the two extremes of cinema. They are the focal points in the ellipsis along which the world of cinema was born, fragmented, and spun out of orbit, with the result that one can no longer speak of cinema. From Dreyer to Straub there is a change of focus. Yet again from Rossellini to Godard. Straub swims against cinema's tide . . . destroying the cultural milieu of the cine-clubs with an overdose of culture [theatre, music, opera] . . . Godard, on the contrary, allows cinema to lose itself in the channels he opens up with his sub-cultural metamorphoses, ranging from militant film to television to video. The extreme points reached by all constitute the spectrum of cinema. Straub the ultraviolet, Godard the infrared, both haunting the space whose limits they exceed, and in which we think we recognize and see ourselves.[117]

JMS and JLG represented cinematographic modernity at its most extreme and opposing points. Straub and Huillet embodied pure resistance at the level of narrative and composition; Godard followed a path of total impurity that incorporated television, video and photography, and juxtaposed sound, text and image. The 'Straubfilm'—the adopted shorthand for the co-works—rebelled at every level, starting with narrative composition; Godard pushed

116 *Cahiers* 260, October 1975.

117 *Cahiers* 264, February 1976; *Cahiers* 258–259, July–August 1975.

for constant recontextualization, he 'forced you to see', whereas the Straubfilm was closer to being, in Daney's phrase, 'a tombstone for the eye'.[118] Godard put on screen our deepest anxieties. We turn on the television, as he showed us in *Number Two*, to 'cheat death every night at home, to avoid seeing our own shadow'.[119] Godard's process of accumulation contrasted with Straub and Huillet's acts of evacuation: film-making that rejects everything spectacular as the great lie of cinema, 'perverse, fascist, pornographic'. By stripping away from within cinema, the Straub-film revealed both the nature of the art, and the world through it; Godard's contrasting technique and practice finally achieved the same opening.

The JLG–JMS axis briefly dictated *Cahiers*' editorial line, and led editors to engage closely with the work of other independent film-makers. In particular, the American Robert Kramer's *Milestones*—as *Ice* had been in 1970—was presented in *Cahiers* as the most important offering from North America when it came out in 1975, and editors arranged a round-table to discuss the film. Kramer's ethnographic portrait of a 1970s America in the shadows of Vietnam and the civil rights movement offered a genuinely original and deeply cinematographic consideration of the composition of political resistance post-1968, in marked contrast with the drab new naturalism or retro style coming from many French directors. Editors praised the film unanimously, largely on criteria established during the Maoist period: Kramer's work was exemplary in its militant content, but the information it conveyed was achieved artistically. Toubiana admired the off-screen space in particular, which evoked the political reality of the US by gesturing towards what was not shown but nonetheless made present in the minds of spectators. By extension, the absence of such debates and considerations in French society was also sharply brought out during the viewing of the film. Kramer was critical of his country's

118 Baecque II, p. 279; for a lucid and illuminating account of Godard's career to date see Michael Witt, 'Shapeshifter', *New Left Review* 29, September–October 2004.

119 This was Serge Le Péron's conclusion in his review of the film, *Cahiers* 262, January 1976.

leaders and their policies in a way that was completely absent from the equivalent cinematic undertakings in France.

Retreat from the margins

Yet the *Milestones* coverage was a swansong to this type of investigation and allegiance to independent works at *Cahiers*. It did not mark the start of a new, reformulated radicalism that allowed at the same time a renewed and passionate cinephilia to express itself. With Kramer, and also Tati and JLG–JMS, the experiment had some life. But scepticism was also rife in the offices, especially amongst those concerned with the magazine's solvency. Toubiana was not convinced this kind of coverage should be leading the editorial line: 'How can we think of ourselves as a minority public against the ideology of cinema which only thinks of the public in majority terms?'[120] Surely there must be some bending to the will of the market? If commercial cinema was not outlawed permanently, there was still the choice over whether engagement should be critical or accommodating.

In March 1976, uncertain, essentially symptomatic reviews of *Jaws* and *Pinocchio* appeared. Returning to Hollywood brought *Cahiers* closer to its approach of the yellow years. Then, of course, the magazine had devoted much attention to addressing popular cinema and works from within the industry. However, doing so in the 1970s required different tools. The nature of the industry was radically different from the Hollywood in which Hawks or Hitchcock had operated: the studios had been broken up and audiences had shifted to the small screen. Contemporary directors could only attract viewers to the film theatres with the promise of something you wouldn't get at home, and in industry terms this meant creating the 'event' film: a production released to great media fanfare simultaneously in every cinema, with a bigger budget, louder soundtrack, more visually arresting scenes and spectacular special effects than its predecessor.

At *Cahiers*, when commercial film returned, there were few

120 *Cahiers* 262, January 1976.

justifications for why, beyond their high profile, these films should receive attention. In truth, Hollywood made its comeback at the magazine for reasons of accumulation and assimilation: we'll write about what people seem to be watching, rather than address readers with our interventions and boldly pit Kramer *against* Spielberg to extrapolate why one should be described and celebrated as an *auteur*, the other a businessman.

Bazin-lite

The pale resurrection of the yellow years' foundations continued apace: first Hollywood's comeback, quickly followed by a mild re-engagement with the ideas of André Bazin. This occurred partly via Deleuze who, as Toubiana later explained, 'took up as essential a history of cinema that Langlois, Bazin, *Cahiers*, Truffaut and Godard had constructed before him'.[121] Deleuze the cinephile conformed to a view the editors already held, rather than providing them with a challenging counter-model.

In this vein, Bonitzer was allowed greater licence to develop his ideas on the aesthetics of cinema. From 1978 onwards he worked to rehabilitate the *mise en scène* as a legitimate concept of analysis, after its disgrace in the years of politicization. His articles for *Cahiers* in the late seventies are considered landmark texts for film theory.[122] Since the sixties Bonitzer had become one of the most consistent critics at the magazine: whatever the chosen editorial line, he intelligently articulated it through his always theoretical and aesthetic approach. In the militant years he worked closely with Comolli to define the true 'political film', contrasting Kramer and Costa-Gavras. In 1974 he collaborated with Daney on his 'critical function' series.

Bonitzer's contribution to the debate however makes clear the gulf between his approach and Bazin's. A key difference in the exploration of aesthetics as enacted by Bonitzer in the seventies, and Bazin twenty

121 Quoted in Dosse, *Gilles Deleuze et Félix Guattari*, 2007, pp. 473 and 475.
122 Reynaud, *Cahiers du cinema, Volume IV*, p. 14.

years before, is the method the two critics used. Less a 'midwife for clear thought', as Bazin had been described,[123] the real object of criticism for Bonitzer was a complex of signifieds not necessarily shown in the frame, which he called 'surplus meaning'. As he saw it, the critic must account for this by speaking in a 'metalanguage'. His role was to add meaning to a film by drawing out its latent content—not unveiling something already there, but constructing ideas that are produced by the work though do not exist within it. Bonitzer was critical of what he saw as the blindness of the *politique* method employed by his predecessors: 'about two decades ago some film critics thought they had discovered such health, such self-assurance and such plenitude in American movies; a cinema without fault or left-over'.[124]

Bonitzer had set up a straw man, simplifying the early engagement with American cinema. Fundamentally reluctant to privilege the director as the supreme locus of meaning. Instead, the critic rose to the fore, legitimating the aesthetic investigations he would carry out around various concepts that were for critics thinking the film, not for engaging in more collective discussions by sharing an experience of watching with other viewers or the director. Daney did not fully subscribe to Bonitzer's approach, retaining the belief that the source of meaning remained within, because film was always something offered by someone else: the critic and the viewer were not the authority.[125]

Bonitzer's texts were couched in an academic and theoretical register that had become increasingly the norm at *Cahiers*, especially when dealing with aesthetic questions. This approach was quite the opposite to Bazin's lucid writing, invigorated by a pedagogical, communicative spirit. Bazin's aim had always been to stick very close to the film, and through his analysis show readers or his cine-club audience the work they *had* seen, but not necessarily fully understood. The game with Bonitzer was motivated primarily by a desire to prove

123 Audience member present at a Bazin cine-club session, quoted in Dudley Andrew, *André Bazin*, p. 95.
124 *Cahiers* 250, May 1974.
125 *Cahiers* 250, May 1974.

the critic's supreme intelligence and ingenuity, his ability to draw out ideas and insights. In this sense, the extent to which Bazin really returned to *Cahiers* in the seventies was only very partial—through individual critics and the closer attention given to formal qualities that had declined during the politicized period. By no means did the Bazinian approach form the backbone of its broader editorial line.

Separate ways

A parallel process occured in later seventies: a still polemical spirit, tinged by hints of concession and disillusion. Editors were spirited and forward-looking as they championed Godard and Straub against Malle's retro style or the new naturalism in French cinema. Daney was the critic with the sharpest tongue and strongest conviction that there was still much at stake in the choice of one film, director or movement over another. Of Robert Altman he remarked: 'what's unpleasant about his films is that the only thing we're asked to admire is the intelligence of the director'. He continued to rail against *Série-Z* films, *1900* or *Illustrious Corpses* which, he argued, attempted to unite a 'median left' audience around 'themes emptied of concrete history' so as not to offend anyone—the anarchist peasant revolts of Emilia-Romagna in *1900* becoming 'a sort of anticipation of the PCI's Historic Compromise'. The process depended on a 'willed amnesia, nourished with images of beauty', like the red flags of the starving peasants. It produced films that were 'vague, reformist, imprecise, unifying, well-intentioned'—but, he asserted, 'cinema should divide': what mattered was 'the idea of risk'. Instead, a new sort of European *cinéma de qualité* would 'set Schlöndorff on Proust, or Losey on Mozart, and think that that's enough.'[126]

This kind of spirit and urgency was progressively becoming the minority position within the *Cahiers* offices. A number of those centrally involved—Toubiana, Narboni, Bonitzer, Alain Bergala and others—were seeking a more comfortable model. 'Why do we give ourselves such a hard time?' Bonitzer asked. 'There seems to be a suspicion of narrative, of the novelistic . . . Nowadays, if anything,

126 Daney, *Maison, 1*, pp. 30 and 25f.; *Maison, 2*, p. 30.

it's the lack of good stories that makes itself felt'. Bergala argued that *Cahiers* had to shed its reputation as a theoretical journal, 'intelligent but austere, or at least not enjoyable'.[127] Toubiana undertook a professionalization of the outfit, driving up subscription figures. At the start of 1981 he boasted, '*Cahiers* has returned as leader of the pack of monthly film magazines', announcing a fixed print run of 20,000. The involvement of the Gaumont media empire as an investor was mooted, although not followed through.[128]

Toubiana envisaged an opening for *Cahiers*, but one that was very different to Rivette's earlier *ouverture*. In the late seventies it was not about further intellectual curiosity or shaking off the shackles of an established, comfortable model to pursue uncharted artistic territory. Rather, the 'vision' was simple dispersal, making *Cahiers* something for everyone, whether this was Godard's cinema or Truffaut's increasingly mainstream fare; the 'dream' was that the two could coexist in the journal—as indeed they did, both interviewed in the October 1980 issue—rather than be juxtaposed against each other. In the same vein, festivals became integral events on *Cahiers*' calendar after Toubiana returned to Cannes in 1977, following the journal's eight-year absence. Two years later, the summer issue was devoted entirely to the Croisette.

There is no specific date for this shift in direction. The process was gradual but the outcome never inevitable. The cracks in the Daney–Toubiana tandem emerged most visibly perhaps in the editorial of 1978, where the turn away from theoretical articles was presaged. The new age of the 'cultural consumer', with cinema's monopoly over mass imagination replaced by that of the *tout-image* of the giant media and advertising corporations, demanded a discourse that aimed not simply to produce opinions and analyses but—the compromise evident in the vagueness of the formulation—'to slice it differently': *découper différemment le cinéma*. This might involve a reworked

---

127 *Cahiers* 281, October 1977; *Cahiers* 287, April 1978. After his early collaboration on *Pierre Rivière*, Bonitzer in particular has devoted much of his time to writing stories. He has provided the screenplay for over thirty films to dates working with Rivette, André Téchiné, Raoul Ruiz and Chantal Ackerman, amongst others. In 1989 he directed his first feature film.
128 Baecque II, pp. 305, 291.

cinephilia, an examination of the film industry, or an increasing amount of information and reportage. At this point came a redesign that increased the journal to 72 pages and opened the way for colour photographs inside. Antoine de Baecque, *Cahiers*' official biographer, reports violent quarrels in the smoke-filled 'end office' over the direction of the journal at this time.[129]

Small screen cinephilia

Daney was increasingly interested in pursuing a new kind of writing and engagement with cinema, namely journalism and the reviewing of films on television. He experimented with this at *Cahiers* initially, through the 'Journals des *Cahiers*' project: a slim newspaper inserted into the pages of the review which appeared every month from January 1980. Its aim was to cover 'a broader and more various selection of cinematic material' in briefer form. The 'Journals' allowed a platform for Jean-Claude Biette and Louis Skorecki, both film-makers as well as critics,[130] to address more closely an issue given little attention in the main magazine: the paradigm shift in the image world accomplished by the triumph of television. Their column was a last gasp of really innovative criticism at *Cahiers* as they sought a new language to register the relationship between both media.[131]

---

129 Baecque II, p. 306.

130 Jean-Claude Biette (1942–2003) had been an infrequent contributor to *Cahiers* since 1964. He was a direct product of the cinephile generation of the early sixties, a regular at the Mac-Mahon, and Cinémathèque screenings. After time in Italy, working with Pasolini and Bertolucci, and directing his own short films, he wrote again for *Cahiers* in the seventies, returning with 'Rewatching *Wichita*' in number 281, a piece on the experience of re-viewing on television Jacques Tourneur's western from 1955. See in particular his *La Poétique des auteurs*, Paris 1988, and *Qu'est-ce qu'un cinéaste*, Paris 2000. Louis Skorecki had been with Daney at the Lycée Voltaire and both joined *Cahiers* in 1963. Skorecki started making films in 1966. He left *Cahiers* for *Libération* at the same time as Daney, and remained at the newspaper until 2007.

131 Further explored by Jonathan Rosenbaum in *Trafic* 37 Spring 2001, pp. 181–192.

Skorecki had already outlined this in his 1966 article 'Against the New Cinephilia', in which he derided those trying to recreate the past glories of the forties and fifties, when cinema provided one of the only substantial external images in people's lives, and discoveries of *auteurs* at the Cinémathèque unleashed great passions and debates. Subsequent generations were engaging with cinema nostalgically, Skorecki argued, when they should instead be taking these changes on board. *Cahiers*, too, was guilty of an old-fashioned cinephilia, and had only responded by replacing criticism with politics and cultural struggle. Yet the only cinephilia now possible was one that engaged with television. For many *Cahiers* editors however, television was a 'sub-culture' (Kané).

Becoming ordinary

Much editorial energy in the last years of the seventies was spent playing catch-up, with America top of the list. The 'Letter from Hollywood' written by man-on-the-ground Bill Krohn was instituted from 1978, establishing for the first time in *Cahiers*' history a permanent connection with the US and its industry's cinema. The July–August 1979 issue led with a shot of Martin Sheen in *Apocalypse Now* on the cover, while Toubiana's editorial introduced, somewhat shamefacedly, a 'scoop' interview with Coppola of astonishing banality (his Oscars and so forth).

As well as opening the door to every new release, *Cahiers* humbly 'discovered' the directors it had ignored during the Maoist regime of JLG–JMS–Eisenstein. This *repêchage* was most fruitful when it turned its attention to Fassbinder at last, and late Bergman, Ozu, Pialat and Tarkovsky.[132] Cinema had been busy, had evolved. But the unexplored masterworks and, with Fassbinder and Pialat, a new generation of *auteurs*, were canonized borrowing the format of the traditional style—a dossier, an interview, a filmography and lots

132 The reception of Fassbinder in particular still remained lacklustre. In 1992 a meagre retrospective appeared, led by Olivier Assayas's praise for one of the director's least impressive works, *Querelle*.

of nice stills—but all this now carried out without controversy or passion. It was slipshod, compared to the once-obsessive rigour that had produced special issues like that on American cinema in 1965. Then, editors had combined the encyclopaedic format with critical lightness of touch, the ability to seize in a crisp paragraph the essence of a director's work. Now, *Cahiers* compromised its high cinephile standards and became more academic and abstract. Pialat's television series *La Maison des bois* was passed over in favour of his later (lesser) Cannes-winning works *Under the Sun of Satan* and *Van Gogh*. The magazine still tried to act the part of the dedicated film rag but stopped bothering with clarifying critical standards. It lavish equal praise on Godard, Ozu, de Palma, Coppola and the 'two Truffauts'.[133]

Fork in the road

The special issues in May and June 1981 to mark *Cahiers*' 30 years were Daney's final contribution as co-editor. He edited the first instalment, Toubiana the second. In them the divergence of paths is clear: Daney's number was full of working ideas and included his carefully selected account of contemporary French cinema, at its best defined by Pialat, Eustache and Garrel; Biette wrote a careful assessment of the long-disregarded Chabrol, characterizing him aptly as 'the man at the centre'. Toubiana's issue by contrast focused entirely on production, the nuts and bolts of film-making, filling the pages with facts and figures. In August Daney left. It was a separation that determined the future of the journal into the eighties and indeed up to today: the split between the two editors marked a fork in the road for *Cahiers*, between balancing on a radical, marginal, cinephile line and occupying the *juste milieu* of a standard glossy monthly.

133 It was in his *Libération* column that Serge Daney made the distinction between the 'two Truffauts': 'Truffaut-Jekyll' and 'Truffaut-Hyde', 'one respectable, the other shady, one keeps things tidy, the other disturbs'. In *The Woman Next Door*, Daney argued that at last the two had met (30 September 1981).

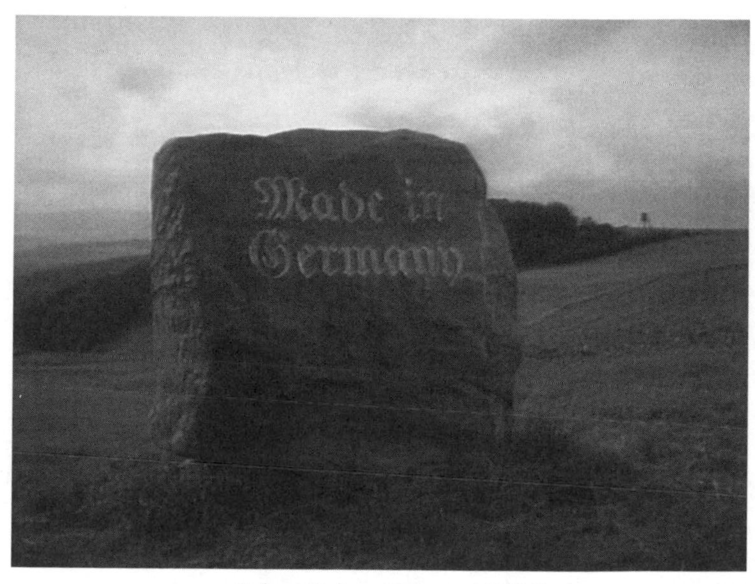

Edgar Reitz, *Heimat 1* (1984)

7

1981–2009

The Mainstream

The radical impulse that animated the choices and interests of the editors, which the red years had pushed to the extreme, continued in some form until 1981. The Daney–Toubiana tandem had overseen a period of rehabilitation at the basic level: getting back some readers, looking and acting like a magazine about cinema, maintaining a regular production cycle. Under the direction of Serge Daney, *Cahiers* had also led a sustained attack on the *fiction de gauche* from Costa-Gavras and French 'new naturalism'; the French retro style manifest in historical dramas, especially those dealing with events in the twentieth century; and dedictated close attention to the works of independent directors such as Robert Kramer and Straub–Huillet.

In this sense, there was no real rupture between the red years and their immediate aftermath; more a shift in emphasis and the acceptance on the part of *Cahiers* editors that they best served the struggle as cinema critics, not political activists. Their passion for film, however much it had been shaken, questioned and embittered, could not be quashed. Let cinephilia live, then, but without excluding politics. Militant activism could instead be channelled through powerfully critical approaches to the art.

In 1981 Serge Toubiana became sole editor-in-chief. Daney went to *Libération* to be their resident film critic, where he would remain for ten years. The tandem broken down, *Cahiers* lost its poet, its thinker, its most passionately cinephile editor. All those who departed in the early or mid-seventies—Comolli, Eisenschitz, Fieschi, Narboni, Pierre—

had not envisaged such an outcome, nor desired it. But they were now engaged elsewhere: Comolli and Fieschi had moved to film-making; Eisenschitz was editing the collected writings of Georges Sadoul; Narboni had become a major influence at Vincennes. That *Cahiers* was now being led by an editor who had arrived at *Cahiers* as a Maoist and been taken on for his apparent political nous rather than his cinephilia was a cruel twist—but all who had once been instrumental in making this story were too distant to intervene anew.

What followed was a period of protracted death for the review: its once *dérangeante* or troublemaking presence became a mouthpiece for the market, bound within the covers of a standard monthly glossy. Its well-intentioned coverage was wider than ever, the style mannered, if curiously affectless; the overall effect—so much to choose from, so little at stake—had, and to this day reproduces, the mind-numbing quality of an up-market consumer report. The closest competitors became *Première*, *Les Inrockuptibles* and *Studio*. There were of course some peaks in the otherwise constant trough: good writers penning interesting articles, a number of fresh, imaginative editors coming on board. But none had any sway over the general direction to reposition *Cahiers* at the centre of the film industry.

At what moment was this irrevocably confirmed; when was the final nail knocked into the coffin? There are various symbolic markers one could choose: the format change in 1978; the cover pictures of Hollywood blockbusters; the change of offices and the new seclusion of editors in their own rooms rather than the single space of the rancho notorious at the Champs-Elysées (where the mail was opened by the first who arrived and critics came in and out constantly, warring or enthusing over the latest release with equal passion); or the vast coverage of *Apocalypse Now Redux* and *Pearl Harbour* in the same issue, one that could only find a few short lines about Rivette's *Va savoir*. Whatever the precise date of its demise, *Cahiers* now is dead.

The last ciné-fils walks away

Irreconcilable differences existed between Daney and Toubiana from the start, though their friction does not fully explain why

Daney left *Cahiers*. The years 1974–81 had really been his, but the approach he took could not promise solvency, nor secure immediate popularity and higher shelf sales. By contrast, 'Toubiana has a very precise idea of what he wants to do with the journal: to relocate it at the cinematic centre. My idea is less clearly defined, more vagabond—but his has a future.'[134] In a 1983 interview with *Esprit*, Daney was diplomatic: some had reproached Toubiana for 'watering the wine' as he moved to put the journal onto a more commercial footing; its current style was a marked retreat from the theoretical ambitions of earlier years. But 'the times themselves have grown more feeble, in terms of thought'.[135]

Daney left because he saw the film critic's critical function in the eighties very differently, but there were a host of other factors. For one, Daney was starting to believe in the 'death of cinema' thesis that had been hanging over the art for so long. The Lumière brothers first mooted it; the decline of Hollywood and finally the universal success of television seemed to confirm it beyond doubt. The era of the *tout image* had to be taken very seriously, it spewed out an eyeful of images—adverts, constantly-running news channels, re-runs of films on cable—within which cinema occupied only a very small part. The special place it once held in our lives, Daney thought, was being so thoroughly obliterated that the magic of the movies existed most vividly in our memories. It was precisely this combination that Daney believed was crucial: the death of cinema and the strong memory of

134 Baecque II, p. 309.

135 Daney, *La Maison cinéma et le monde 2. Les Années Libé (1981–1985)*, Paris 2002, 2, p. 19. Relations between Daney and Toubiana remained friendly. Daney did not speak derisively of the journal, and he continued to contribute pieces over the years. But in 1991 a major break occurred after Daney wrote a negative review of Claude Berri's *Uranus* in *Libération*. Daney had been hurt by the paper's unprecedented decision to allow the director right of reply, yet none of his colleagues, nor any amongst the wider circle of critics—Toubiana included—came out in support of Daney, something that left him feeling deeply isolated. The thaw came in 1992, when Daney accepted Toubiana's proposal to conduct a long interview as a last attempt to assemble something like a *ciné-biographie* of Daney before his death. This became the posthumously published *Persévérance*.

the art of film. But *Cahiers* would not accept such a radical cut. Instead it would be accommodating: accept everything as cinema and cover it all. Yet writing for the review continued, now pointlessly, to demand that critics adopt the 'we' register, invoke an *esprit de chapelle* long-since departed from the office, and use a style that referred to film in a way that did not take account of these changes, and therefore seemed mannered, overly stylized, in denial of the times.

Daney felt he had to address what he saw as a paradigm shift in the art: most subsequent generations will first experience cinema on the small screen, as the movie theatres stand as relics or museums more than vibrant secular churches. He had to find a way to write on cinema that managed to communicate its history at the same time as engage with its present. The critic could not be satisfied with writing 'on a worthwhile novelty opening to an empty hall', he must also deal with a re-run on television, seen by millions. 'Time has passed for my generation', he would later explain, 'and it is tempting to write for the section of *Libération*'s readership that is twenty, that doesn't know, and to whom one would like to transmit the feeling that all this has already existed for others before them'.[136]

Daney's move was, therefore, motivated in large part by the desire for transmission. Inspired by Bazin's example before him—Daney effectively became more Bazinian as time went on—he saw daily journalism as one means of meeting this pedagogical ambition.[137] *Libération* offered freedom of expression (he never had to toe any editorial line until the *Uranus* controversy) and a wide readership. He was attracted by the idea of penning an article on the quick,

136 Daney, *Devant la recrudescence des vols de sacs à main*, p. 6.

137 Like Bazin, Daney was reluctant to pursue this within an institution. Daney did teach at Censier, but never with much vocational enthusiasm for the role of professor. Bazin had noted his own reservations at such a method for transmitting film understanding in his critical account of the Institut de Filmologie at the Sorbonne, which opened in 1948 and counted Labarthe and Godard as early—though far from regular—attendees. For Bazin, the method of work at this institution amounted to a plundering of the insights gleaned from film and critical writing on it and reincorporating them into the disciplines of philosophy or sociology.

which would appear once and then might serve to 'wrap the fish' the following day. It was simple, and also aleatory: there was a good chance that people would engage with his thoughts, deepen their understanding of cinema, but as a natural extension of their lives and reflections. *Libération* was a daily, it was disposable and Daney could write incognito—all attributes that contrasted completely with the historic import placed on contributing to *Cahiers* each month. *Libération* did not offer a place in which to write words that would be recorded in the archives, but it promised to bring the critic closer to the world of cinema as it was being made, and closer to its audiences.

Watering the wine: the French Left in the 1980s

Why could this critical project not be realized from within, through an internal transformation of *Cahiers* in the spirit of previous demolitions and renewals that had characterized its life cycle up to this point? Daney's aspirations clashed not only with Toubiana's more viable, level-headed proposal, but also with the spirit of the day.

Cahiers' turn towards the mainstream can really only be understood in the context of the broader patterns of French intellectual culture at the time. Writing in the *London Review of Books* in 2004, Perry Anderson has anatomized the concerted ideological and institutional campaign, initially mobilized against the threat of a United Left victory, that was spearheaded by a phalanx of liberal intellectuals (François Furet, Pierre Nora, Pierre Rosanvallon, to name a few) at this time. Working through media such as *Débat*, *Nouvel Observateur* and *Esprit*, the academy—notably the Rockefeller-funded Ecole des Hautes Etudes en Sciences Sociales, and the Fondation Saint-Simon, gathering-place for business and political elites—remade the country's ideological landscape between the mid-seventies and the bicentenary of 1789. The 'normalization' of French culture in line with prevailing Atlanticist winds could draw in part on the new-found anti-Gulagism of former Maoists now influential in the media. These post-sixties movers and shakers contributed their own feel-good style to the project—a sense that their embrace of the free-market system was the radicalism *du jour*. The 'left' was no longer to be defined by its critique of capitalism, but in terms of inoffensive values like justice or generosity. A new 'libertarian–neoliberal' tone characterized debates and writing—'plugged-in', flippant, eternally young—that with Mitterrand's victory in 1981 became the lingua franca of a smart and stylish post-socialism.

The 1980s marked the rapid disillusion of any remaining hopes for the Left in the face of its crumbling organized channels. Various factors combined to create an environment that was hostile to the free exploration and critique of cinema outside the market logic. Mitterrand had promised radical reformism, but this pledge was quickly abandoned after two years, when the Socialist Party adopted a technocratic, non-class approach to the management ('with a human face') of French capitalism. Reform made way for modernization: France must 'streamline', 'rationalize' and 'technologize' itself to raise its 'international status'—a lexicon that even the French Right had not dared to use. Mitterrand became one of President Reagan's strongest supporters in matters of foreign policy, whilst Culture Minister Jack Lang defended the *exception culturelle* at home.

The remarkably successful campaign by ex-Maoists and *soixante-huitards* for a repentant anti-Gulagism dramatically changed the political discourse of the French Left. By 1988, when Mitterrand campaigned for re-election, Marxism, class-analysis perspectives, and voices for socialist transition, equality and anti-capitalism were all silent. The Socialists reached out to the centre with promises of market flexibility, competitiveness and appeals to the logic of international economics. As George Ross and Jane Jenson observed at the time, 'the old Left discourse—in which the gap between ambitious political goals and the constraints of the real world appeared as a problem that could be resolved through voluntaristic determination—was overwhelmed . . . Real-world constraints were elevated to rigid boundaries of the possible.'[138]

138 George Ross and Jane Jenson, 'The Tragedy of the French Left', *New Left Review*, 1/171, September–October 1988, p. 14.

This was essentially the logic behind the Toubiana years at *Cahiers*. The result was the dual activity of covering both mainstream and independent cinema, in full-colour format. American blockbusters were given dedicated coverage (*Batman* on the cover in September 1981 was one of the emblematic moments of Toubiana's editorial takeover). The boundaries of the possible had reduced significantly; market-driven models were presented as the only projects to hold out much potential shelf-life. *Cahiers* must seek out a wider public, and it would do this by becoming more palatable to the busy consumer-reader.

Articles offering more profound and challenging considerations of cinema, or surveying developments on the margins of the industry, were slowly becoming extinct. Raymond Bellour's appraisal of Thierry Kuntzel's video work, for example, in March 1981—commissioned by Daney for one of the final issues in his charge—would be unthinkable in *Cahiers* only a few years later. The wonderful two-part series on the genesis of a new 35mm camera, by Jean-Pierre Beauviala and Godard, ran over two issues in 1983. Increasingly, however, such space was instead given over to the latest Hollywood productions, or to star-gazing at Isabelle Huppert and Gérard Depardieu as though these *vedettes* merited yet more attention.[139] The rhythm of *Cahiers* was the market, its heartbeat was distributors—whatever is out there, whatever the industry wants us to see—and in only impoverished form was attention cast quickly to what was being made but not necessarily exhibited. *Cahiers* effectively entered 'reality'; it got wise to the consensus and treated film as part of the same world, rather than a world apart.

Evolutions in French cinema

A number of new movements and styles came out of French cinema in the eighties. A young *cinéma d'auteur* was emerging from the latest crop of IDHEC graduates;[140] heritage films that adapted Pagnol

139 In 1994, Isabelle Huppert edited *Cahiers* 477.

140 Founded in 1944, the Institut des Hautes Etudes Cinématographiques (expanded in 1985 and renamed La Fémis) is responsible for schooling a large majority of France's directors. Of the generation to emerge in the eighties: Arnaud Desplechin, Patrice Leconte, André Téchiné. In the nineties:

or Zola novels, and were strongly subsidized and promoted by the Culture Ministry; and what became known as a *cinéma du look*, stylized but vacant films from more commercially-minded directors such as Luc Besson. These various styles and tendencies required that *Cahiers* choose their camp, though this was done with far more diplomacy than before.

Auteurs everywhere

The *auteur* had become banalized quickly. Already in 1962, Godard had noted that rather too many were being granted the title; 'inflation threatens', he warned—but in the eighties the process was institutionalized. Jack Lang expanded and restructured the Parisian film school through which most already passed in order to 'learn the trade'. By means of the Culture Ministry's *politique de prestige du cinéma*, the object—the *auteur* film—was invented, and then presented as something in need of protection, with its own set of subsidies and preservation policies. In 1989 Lang enforced laws that required the majors to increase their programming of so-called *œuvres fragiles*. Such policies and economic subsidies encouraged budding film-makers to think of the *auteur* as a role anyone could step into from the beginning. In order to receive funds they voluntarily appropriated the label, rather than being designated as worthy of it after critical judgement and a number of completed films.[141]

The 'Lang years'—a period when cinema was literally '*mis en scène*', placed on stage—were noted at *Cahiers*, though when editors took stock in March 1986 the response was a bureaucratic

---

Jean-Jacques Annaud, Laurent Cantet, Claire Denis. From previous generations: Louis Malle, Costa-Gavras and Alain Resnais.

141 In a round table on young French cinema in 1993, various new directors discussed terms and concepts in the industry. Around *auteur* the team stated they felt 'ambivalence', that there was a risk of 'asphyxiation by the "I" or "me"' in this approach, but all agreed 'the notion is at the centre of young French cinema. Today one cannot enter into film-making without being one, and a good thing too.' *Cahiers* 473, November 1993.

alphabet list of the various reforms and new vocabulary that had sprung up as a result of the economic, structural and policy changes. The institutionalization of the *auteur* figure by outsiders was resented, and yet *Cahiers* itself did little to reclaim it by attending to the deeper implications of the term (as highlighted by Bazin) or carrying forward the extensive groundwork the concept required. This would have meant developing a better grasp of all types of cinematic language, challenging the meaning of the *mise en scène*, judging the significance of elements not controlled by the director, and extrapolating on the way a director works and how this translates to the finished result. At *Cahiers*, editors instead followed the expansion route, enlarging the now catch-all term. The *auteur* notion—the journal's notion, its real house concept—was bandied about indiscriminately, pinned to every Pierre, Paul, Jacques and found everywhere.

Skin deep

The so called *cinéma du look* developed in the eighties and nineties was led by directors keen to produce a domestic equivalent to the Hollywood blockbuster. Its name derived from the slick visual style of the films, borrowed unashamedly from techniques used in advertising. Masters of the genre were Luc Besson, Jean-Jacques Beineix and Leos Carax, with films such as *Subway*, *Nikita*, *The Big Blue*, *Betty Blue* and *The Lovers on the Bridge*. At *Cahiers* the movement was strongly condemned and the associated directors chastised as producers of 'readymades' that regurgitated the pop videos and television clips currently 'in the air'.[142] Alain Bergala disparagingly described the films as 'mannerist': every resource had been exhausted, the style of *look* films was confused, replete with inert myths and dependent on a fake, amnesiac cinephilia which was nothing but an offshoot of television broadcasting.[143]

142 Serge Toubiana quoted in Phil Powrie, *French Cinema in the 1980s: Nostalgia and the Crisis of Masculinity*, Oxford 1991, p. 7.
143 Bergala, *Cahiers* 370 and 353, April 1985 and November 1983.

Yet Carax was singled out as an exception. His second film (*The Night is Young*, a self-indulgent love story told in a series of breathless snatches) puts one in mind of a second-rate Godard in his *Pierrot le fou* days. Yet this was an 'absolute dazzler' according to Alain Philippon, showing 'mind-blowing virtuosity'.[144] Carax was familiar to *Cahiers* since his days there as a critic in the early eighties, and appealed largely because his work evinced a degree of film-historical consciousness. Though this manifests more as mere imitation in the films themselves, editors preferred to see cinematic tributes, and appreciated the distinctive *mise en scène* and recurring themes.

Thierry Jousse, in a round-up of the state of French cinema in 1989, discerned some common traits in recent works. On the negative side, he found many films were incapable of figurative representation.[145] 'What would a foreigner, with no idea of French cinema past or present, think if suddenly he stumbled upon its actors, movie theatres and streets?' Jousse asked. He would find 'an absence, a hole, a gap', whose name was 'the real, considered impossible by an ironic, Lacanian cinema'. The real, reality, realism: all had been evacuated from French cinema.[146] This was, Jousse explained, a result of the postmodern, post-industrial context in which these films were being made. Luc Besson's scuba diver saga *The Big Blue* was about nothing more than a formal concept—the monochromic variation on pure colour—and followed its protagonist in his journeys to the bottom of the ocean by registering on the image itself a fusion with the blue, the result being 'the literal disappearance of the figure inside a universe without purpose, unfathomable'.[147]

The sources of hope were found with the young *auteur* cinema, that of Arnaud Desplechin, André Téchiné, Olivier Assayas and Philippe Garrel. In similarly uninspiring terms to the canonization of Carax, André Téchiné was admired for dedicating his œuvre to fiction, to telling a good yarn. This was all the more laudable because

---

144 *Cahiers* 389, November 1986.
145 *Cahiers* 419–420, May 1989.
146 *Cahiers* 428, February 1990.
147 *Cahiers* 419–420, May 1989.

as a former *Cahiers* critic he was fully aware that the age of innocent storytelling *à la* Hitchcock or Lang had passed. But Téchiné was commended for taking the basics of great Hollywood cinema and personalizing them with his particular landscapes and faces. Téchiné's wager was that cinema had indeed lost its innocence, but that 'it has more to gain from remembering this than from trying to forget'.

Really, Téchiné was making banal dramas with recognizable French actors in idyllic settings. A crime affecting a family usually unravelled years of hurt, angst or trauma. At no point did characters grasp the real that Jousse had found absent in Besson. Yet *Cahiers* writers were generally moved by his self-conscious fidelity to fiction. His carefully plotted but preposterous *The Scene of the Crime* was described by Philippon as the film we had all been dreaming of: 'fierce and violent, fast and lyrical, a film that leaves its mark indelibly on our memory'. With Téchiné's film, 'that dream has been realized'; it was a 'pure masterpiece' that played a 'fundamental' role in cinema for the 'few directors who continue to live cinema, and for us too'. In a formulation that read like the instructions in a primary-school textbook, Téchiné was extolled for 'proposing a strange contract with his spectator: know that what you see on the screen is just fiction and, following from this, rediscover faith in the story that unravels before your eyes'. The standards required for greatness had dropped considerably.

The nemesis returns

Heritage productions, that started to appear in the eighties to wide popular acclaim, were championed as the pinnacle of the country's cinematic achievements. Many projects received generous state funding and support. Berri's Pagnol and Zola adaptations, or Jean-Paul Rappenau's *Cyrano de Bergerac* were defended by the Culture Ministry and press alike, partly in an attempt to overturn the perceived 'Americanization' of French cinema, with the percentage share of French/US films in France having tipped in favour of North America since 1987. Heritage films were home-grown blockbusters, promoted to fight the industry battle against Hollywood, which borrowed everything from the US model: make a film so spectacular that viewers feel they must see it on the big screen, because the visual extravaganza cannot be reproduced at home.

The *Germinal* affair in 1993 was a good example of heritage cinema being brandished as a paragon of French invention, against American invaders. Berri's historical drama was released at the same time as *Jurassic Park*—coinciding with the GATT negotiations that were held up by French protectionism—and the clash produced a patriotic defence of Berri's peasants against Spielberg's dinosaurs. *Germinal* was quintessentially French: an adaptation of the original Zola novel and starring crowd favourites Depardieu and Miou-Miou. Going to see the film was mediatized as an act of national pride and support. Jack Lang did his bit: the premiere was government-sponsored and the Culture Ministry had copies sent to schools around the country, as a vital contribution to children's 'national education'.

Heritage cinema received mostly unfavourable coverage at *Cahiers*, with 'authentic' young *auteur* cinema upheld instead. Yet given that the equivalent big-budget films coming from the US were taken perfectly seriously, this opposition was barely credible. And some lukewarm praise did filter through. Toubiana, for example, admired the actors in *Jean de Florette*, concluding diplomatically that 'we can always dream of a film that takes more risks, is more vibrant, and has more stamina', but Berri's effort was 'no less honourable' in the end, given its 'strength of conviction, the respect showed to the text, the sober cinematography—all succeed in making it live'.[148] The verdict would have scandalized the young Truffaut.

The 'movie brats'

The results of *Cahiers*' relocation at the cinematic centre, in terms of film culture and intellectual standards, have been disastrous. The critical questions in cinema were left half-addressed or not at all, as restless heterogeneity snowballed to render the editorial line incoherent. Having taken, as Fredric Jameson has outlined, a turn to

148 *Cahiers* 387, September 1986.

'paranoid' cinema, the renewed Hollywood industry in the nadir of the Reagan era was covered by *Cahiers* with no critical trenchancy. It made for better sales figures to find *auteurs* in abundance operating there. The generation of 'movie brats'—those directors brought up on Ford, Fuller, Hawks and Preminger, along with the New Wave, neo- and poetic realism, and educated in their trade at the proliferating film schools—were hailed in completely inflated terms as revitalized expressions of the industry. Even the remaining serious writers and older editors fell into line. After beatifying Coppola in the eighties, Oudart ushered Kubrick's *The Shining* into the canon, calling it 'a work of great culture—a culture that is not yet dead'. Bonitzer was awed by the 'Dostoevskyan sensibility' of Scorsese's *Raging Bull*, while Narboni enthused over the 'maturity' of *E.T.*: 'intelligent, inventive, moving, mischievous . . . this film should win Spielberg a nomination for the Nobel Peace Prize'.[149]

Cahiers had of course always mixed popular appeal and elitism. From the beginning it had been chastised precisely for elevating 'entertainers' to geniuses. But the riches now discerned in the predictable narratives and merchandise mountains of films such as *E.T.* were of a very different character to the Hitchcocko-Hawksians' analyses. Since the sixties, Hollywood had been separating into an old guard and a transitory new guard, until the Lucas and Spielberg generation destabilized the industry and placed it on a new set of foundations. The process was akin to the crisis of classical Fordism and its replacement by a post-Fordist industry, a reorganization of the institution and its production process. The movie brats ushered in a kind of 'reactionary modernism': at film school they were 'taught' cinephilia in the lecture hall and received a broader cinematic culture from re-runs on television. Innovative and experimental work was initially visible in early Scorsese and Kubrick, for example, but en masse this generation accepted the terms of the game: earn more with each new film, and tailor the work almost exclusively to please the youth market. Over time this has resulted in a repetitive cycle of variations on the same high-tech, speed-and-action, in-your-face

149 *Cahiers* 342, December 1982.

thriller, heart-warming tear-jerker or rom-com. *Star Wars* was *The Sound of Music* all over again.[150]

This new crop of American film-makers revered the New Wave as much as their own past masters (the young Spielberg carried a copy of Fuller's post-war submarine pursuit of A-bombs, *Hell and High Water*, in his car boot for good luck), which allowed a veneer of cinephilia to soften the edges of their Oscar-targeted extravaganzas. *Cahiers* followed the movie brats closely; for market laws, after all, required it to communicate with a broader public. Indeed, rather than cut through the advertising jargon, as it demanded from the *look* film-makers, *Cahiers* reproduced it in a higher register when writing about Hollywood, or replaced it with commentary in the cultural studies mould.[151] Reviews were not always without insight, but the sense of urgency that had animated *Cahiers* from its inception, of conscious struggle against the existing state of things, had gone. The aim was now consolidation, a purely informational investigation of the world as it is, the complete shift from conceiving of film as art to film as culture.

---

150 Peter Wollen, 'Afterword: Lee Russell interviews Peter Wollen', *Signs and Meanings in the Cinema*, London 1998.

151 This model derived from the discipline first developed in 1961 at the Birmingham Centre for Contemporary Cultural Studies in Britain, founded by Richard Hoggart and Stuart Hall. The centre gave institutional form to the approach developed in Hoggart's *The Uses of Literacy* (1957) and Raymond Williams's *Culture and Society* (1958), in which both thinkers presented 'culture' as a way of life that gives texture and meaning to social existence, and avowed their suspicion of commercialized mass culture. Art produced within mass culture was always and only an expression of it, and the appropriate critique, according to this logic, was one that denied such works any aesthetic value—classic Hollywood for example. The risk inherent in this assumption is to undermine notions of artistic autonomy, making it impossible for the critic to tell a masterpiece from the rest. Though *Cahiers*' roots pre-dated the Birmingham School, cultural studies had become a popular interpretive and critical framework for film writing by the eighties. When *Cahiers*' foundations were reconceived, cultural studies filled the gap in partial form.

Critic as channel-hopper

Cinema and television were no longer two separate industries locked in an intense struggle for viewers, as had been the case since the arrival of television into the mass market of the sixties. A mutual dependence had developed, born from logic and necessity: the archive of films offered network programmers ready-made content; in return, film had a new source of distribution and exhibition, which could be further exploited through VHS rental and sales. In 1986, 950 films were screened on French television, a number that had increased to 1,330 two years later. More channels were launched, increasing demand and screening opportunities. More significantly still, television in return became a prime investor in film.

This relationship between the two mediums had been in place in the US since the break-up of the studio era, and had extended to West Germany, Britain, Italy and Spain by the eighties. The cinema–television symbiosis took hold in France with the arrival in 1985 of Canal Plus, a subscription channel devoted almost entirely to films. In 1986 Mitterrand privatized two broadcast channels, including the main TFI; so began the real era of cut-throat competition to pull in audiences and profits. The result was a greater demand for American imports, but Jack Lang also established a tax shelter system that required television to invest a percentage of its income into film production. Canal Plus was the most significant player, its investment doubling to 40 per cent by 1988. The channel could show the films it had co-produced after eleven months, but otherwise was forced to wait the obligatory three years; the motivation was thus to invest in more co-productions. This model is firmly in place in France today, according to which both mediums coexist and support each other.[152]

152 In 2002 the owner of Canal Plus, Vivendi Universal, was brought to near-bankruptcy. The scandal that provoked the crisis circulated largely around the role played by Chief Executive Jean-Marie Messier, and had little final impact on the television–cinema co-operation. The health of this relationship has, however, been in question again, with a downturn in the popularity of films screened on television and a simultaneous rise in cinema attendance recorded in 2004 and 2006.

In practice, therefore, television has become very closely involved in cinema's production and exhibition, provoking speculative concerns across the spectrum of film critics over whether this might lead to a 'televisualization' of cinema, something that was anticipated with gloom at *Cahiers*. Toubiana felt it best to cordon off one from the other: films on the small screen impeded 'what is basic to cinema: the encounter between an *auteur* and a subject. Cinema must have its own temporality: a tempo which is different from the one dictated by media "culture"'.[153]

Now operating outside the *Cahiers* orbit, Daney provided the more incisive engagement with the medium, especially through his hundred-day, one-man marathon beween 1987–88 when he watched TV and chronicled his reactions and reflections for *Libération*.[154] He sat through talk shows, sports coverage, news programmes and movie reruns, concluding that there was such a thing as a distinctive, televisual *mise en scène*, however it might resemble a cemetery full of phantoms floating around tombstones. The *zappeur* or channel-hopper was one who wants to be everywhere at once, flicking between channels in case he misses something, never wanting to lose the fragile thread of any story. But he never takes the risk to stick with just one thing, and so sees nothing. Old movies screened in the dead hours of night made Daney feel that these films were 'pimping themselves', turning up in dark alleys 'dressed up to the nines in hopes of being picked up by one wandering, bored, sleepless viewer'.[155] Watching films on television was not always such a disaster, however. One morning he found, 'drowned amongst other images', Woody Allen's *Zelig*, which allowed him to appreciate many qualities that had not been noticeable in the movie theatre. Viewing *Zelig* on television was to see it 'in its correct environment', because although Allen's works were nearly

153 Toubiana quoted in Phil Powrie, *French Cinema in the 1990s: Continuity and Difference*, Oxford 1999, p. 4.

154 These pieces were later collected and published in *Le Salaire du zappeur*, Paris 1993. The title alludes to Henri-Georges Clouzot's *Le Salaire de la peur*—the wages of fear.

155 Daney's description came during an interview in July 1989 with Olivier Assayas, on Daney's radio show *Microfilms* for France Culture.

always based on strong ideas, 'they rarely have the stamina to make a real film'.[156]

Millennium march

In 1989 the *Cahiers* design was 'aired' to make it more 'visible' and 'readable', which meant more white spacing on the page, more film stills and larger subheadings. It also ensured the review would hold its own physically against *Première* and *Studio* on newsagents' stands. The change reflected a concept of the reader as a busy Parisian on the metro, wanting snappier prose and with very little time to indulge in the kind of articles that required, in Toubiana's condescending phrase, the 'reading pace of a cruise ship'.[157] This switch to a standard magazine formula signalled, in the most blatant fashion, the editors' acknowledgement of targets detached from cinema, namely the attraction of 50,000 readers per issue—the benchmark of a successful glossy.

With this basic aim, the outlook of the review and its relationship to readers was altered once more. Toubiana was moulding *Cahiers* to fit a marketing department's notion of the public—the busy, fleetingly curious, Friday-night film-goer who was a sucker for a pretty photograph. Editors must write to please, advise and pique curiosities, but never to convince of a new idea or to overturn a prejudice. Previously the *guerre de papier* with *Positif* had involved debates over worthy *auteurs*, aesthetic criteria and the tension between politics and art in the critical domain. But other film magazines were now rivals in a simple number-crunching competition: who could pull in the most readers? To be 'cool' and appeal to as many interests as possible, new faces covered all bases—MC Solaar was one new discovery, inexplicably hailed as 'the Jacques Tati of rap'.[158] Following the catch-all policy, the avant-garde and independent developments in cinema were not ignored.

---

156 *Salaire du zappeur*, pp. 57–9.
157 *Cahiers* 425, November 1989, Editorial.
158 *Cahiers* 483, September 1994.

With a non-cinephile logic at work behind *Cahiers*, the two could easily coexist: tough market realism hand-in-hand with trendy radical spirit. Toubiana treated cinema like the product in any other business venture: he followed the money, the influence, the power—all the while careful to talk the talk of dedicated cinephilia.

Toubiana's longue durée

What is particularly telling about Toubiana's editorship is the duration of his tenure. Historically, generations of editors had renewed themselves every five or six years, and the trend continued when Daney left in 1981. Toubiana, however, remained in place for two decades. He was seconded in brief spells by Thierry Jousse, Antoine de Baecque and Charles Tesson. Toubiana was always present however, retaining overall control and ensuring that at no point did any of these editors pursue too seriously more unorthodox, that is to say risky, interests and directions at *Cahiers*. That Toubiana stayed so long at the helm certainly signals, above all, a certain rigidification, an ebbing of the critical tide and, with it, the polarizing polemics that had split and reconstituted editorial boards in the past.

The team Toubiana had inherited in 1981—among them Pascal Kané, Olivier Assayas and Laurent Perrin—was very diverse; other contributors were drawn mainly from the universities—Serge Le Péron at Vincennes, Carax and Tesson at Censier—or were journalists working at current-affairs papers: Bergala and Ignacio Ramonet from *Le Monde diplomatique*, Jean-Paul Fargier from *Tribune socialiste* and *Cinéthique*. Past editors, including Comolli and Douchet, also wrote again for the magazine, and both Daney and Narboni were invited to contribute on many occasions as gestures to serious cinephilia were deftly made. Overall, much of *Cahiers*' contents came from academics and journalists used to writing on a wide number of subjects, while the genuinely film-obsessed critics or practitioners were in the minority—few, in other words, motivated by the desire to engage with film in order to then go on and make it, reinvent it. *Cahiers* was no longer at the frontline. With the contents dictated by the media and industry calendar—whatever else happens in May, we devote our issue to Cannes, and so on—the opposition to, or celebration of particular works was more detached. Passionate partisanship would no longer determine what led an issue, or split editors and audiences: there was no 'dying on the barricades to defend Hitchcock', in Comolli's description of cinephilia,[159] no lofty ambitions to overturn the consensus and rethink assumptions or challenge industry rules.

When Toubiana officially stepped down in 2000, he went on to manage the book and DVD wing of *Cahiers*' publisher, Editions de l'Etoile. Since then he has risen to the top rung of the French cinema industry, becoming director of the Cinémathèque. In 2005 the institution opened different doors to those Henri Langlois had presided over until his death in 1977, as the new venue designed by Frank Gehry was unveiled. As part of Mitterrand's original plans to decentralize culture in Paris, the Cinémathèque's space-age glass structure is located in an eerie no-man's-land far down the rue de Bercy, next to the sports stadium. Toubiana's trajectory as Maoist militant now installed at Bercy is—alongside that of Marin Karmitz, whom Nicholas Sarkozy recently named head of the French government's 'Council of Artistic Creation'—one of the most complete metamorphoses in the cinema circle, an ex-figure from the French Left.

Le Monde moves in

The solvency of Toubiana's model was starting to falter by the time he left at the start of the millennium: monthly sales had dropped to 26,700. The previous year a deal had been met with *Le Monde* publishing group to buy the magazine. This started a new editorial cycle: journalists from the newspaper were shipped in to control *Cahiers*. First came Franck Nouchi, who described the buyout as an act 'to save the world's greatest film magazine'—an explanation striking for its inanity and detachment from a critical

159 Personal communication, January 2009.

project of any sort, and encapsulating the nostalgic terms by which *Cahiers* had come to define itself.

The format was altered to include more coverage of video, DVD and industry news. During this period Jean-Marc Lalanne—who has since become editor of *Les Inrockuptibles*—steered *Cahiers* into covering every possible type of multimedia, from computer games to pornography. Lalanne was also a leading voice in the fawning reception of *Loft Story* (the French equivalent of the reality shows *Big Brother* or *The Real World*), as passions in front of the small screen were reinvigorated by the series—a real low point in the review's recent history. Sales continued to fall, with circulation down to 12,000 in 2002, a drop of 13 per cent on the previous year, followed by a further drop of 11 per cent in 2003. *Le Monde* considered shutting down the review altogether, but opted instead for another editorial change, once more sending in one of their own: Jean-Michel Frodon.

Under Frodon, a standard issue is put together by a team of around ten permanent staff. At nearly a hundred pages, it is split into four sections: the monthly 'Evènement', usually an interview, a retrospective or film festival; the '*Cahiers* critique' or review section, the meat of the whole magazine; the 'Journal', no longer a mini-newspaper, but a functional events listing and collection of reports from conferences and festivals, updates on new film projects, obituaries; and 'Répliques', a random collection of short articles on or around cinema by theorists, critics or film specialists, and some DVD reviews. Interesting writers and worthy pieces continue to appear, but it remains clear that as an intellectual project *Cahiers* is finished, a victim of the same listless market realism on display in a 2000 interview with Toubiana in *Débat*. Only the American industry had been able to keep pace with the changing nature of audiences, the former editor insisted; it had far more money and was better at the re-invention of genres. In Europe, 'what is there new to say?'[160] This was a businessman in bleak mood about his product and, considering what the *Cahiers* radar picked up, his outlook seemed confirmed: the

160 *Le Débat* 112, November–December 2000, p. 168.

Pollyanna-ish *Amélie* for example, merely inspired comparisons with *Shrek* and *Tomb Raider*'s Lara Croft.[161]

Digital horizons?

By 2007 *Cahiers* was shifting 23,000 copies a month, and losing 700,000 euros a year. This was despite attempts at rejuvenation through more format changes and bureaucratic and presentational tweaks. The size of the review was reduced to a 'more manageable' just under A4; a sister publication was launched in Spain, along with an online English version. But in 2008 *Cahiers* and its publisher were put up for sale. The event provoked a number of offers, including an internal proposition from Emmanuel Burdeau, then deputy editor, and Thierry Lounas, a member of the editorial board. Their manifesto for change was the only in-house alternative, and when it was published in *Libération* on 17 July over one hundred colleagues, directors and intellectuals gave their support. Jean Douchet was the first signatory, followed by a number of past editors and fellow travellers including Comolli, Labarthe, Narboni, Pierre, Rancière and Slavoj Žižek.

For Burdeau and Lounas, the future of the review was digital. *Cahiers* must broaden its scope to cover all technologies having an effect on film, especially DVD and the internet. The website should become integral and critics should convey 'how the web at once transforms the way cinema is made and criticism is written and received'. This could lead to more blogs and online reportage. Militant action was also encouraged: critics should actively support the films they admire: 'they must change their job description to become fully-fledged distributors over the internet, on DVD and in the cinemas'.[162]

Does digital really command the cinematic horizon? The Burdeau–Lounas proposal was in its early stages, claiming only that 'the presence

---

161 *Cahiers* 564, January 2002, Editorial.

162 Emmanuel Burdeau and Thierry Lounas, 'Pour des "*Cahiers*" de plaisir et de combat', *Libération*, 17 July 2008.

of digital and its effects are more diffuse'. But they believed that digital 'offers the ideal critical tool' for bringing together cinema 'in its totality', understood as its economy, aesthetics, filming techniques, modes of reception, its great *auteurs* and its avant-garde. Some of the previous market realism was present: their vision was 'a publishing project, but also a business venture. The two are indissoluble. Indeed, the new challenges facing criticism clearly cannot be separated from the new ways forward'.

The venture was neither radical nor especially substantial in the first instance; its questions were all open-ended. Yet it was at least a move against the stranglehold that journalism—the form implanted by *Le Monde*—had over *Cahiers*; and also a stand against academia, whose approach to cinema too often overlooked the necessity of winning an argument or changing mindsets, exposing assumptions and communicating with a non-specialist viewer. Competent journalism and abstract academia constituted *Cahiers*' editorial makeup and Burdeau by contrast was one of the few remaining cinephiles. Thierry Lounas also worked as a film producer.

The proposal and sale mobilized passions within Parisian critical cinephile circles: there was a tangible sense that the future of *Cahiers* was in the balance, with interest shown from rivals *Les Inrockuptibles*, and previous editor and director of *Première* Alain Kruger. Those who signed their names to the letter to 'save *Cahiers*' were moved to do so largely for the sake of the name, and what it evoked in spirit. If *Cahiers* went over to *Première*, or shut down definitively, it could be the beginning of a metastasis which would lead to other reviews perishing too.[163] Most such well-wishers accepted that *Cahiers* had not occupied a leading role since the late seventies, and all could name the moment when *Cahiers* expired as an active intellectual and artistic project. But in a more nostalgic spirit of cinephilia, the Burdeau–Lounas proposal took wind and almost took control. Just as an agreement had been reached between *Le Monde* and the young *Cahiers* editors, their financier backed out. In its place came the English art publisher Phaidon. In November 2008, Editions de

163 Sylvie Pierre, personal communication, January 2009.

l'Etoile was dissolved. Burdeau left shortly afterwards, and Frodon followed in July 2009. At the time of writing no new editor is in place.

An English enterprise at the helm seems an aberration, given *Cahiers*' distinctly French heritage and style. But Filipacchi had hardly been the most appropriate owner in 1964, and editors dealt triumphantly with his reign. Back then there had been a project to fight for, however, whereas the Burdeau–Lounas bid would have saved only the husk of *Cahiers*. In all the speculation around the sale and identity of *Cahiers*' buyer, a *Libération* reporter described the office as a 'haunted house' and ran a double spread with images of the *Cahiers jaunes*, André Bazin, and an old group photo of Daney, Doniol-Valcroze, Narboni, Rohmer and Toubiana.[164] This confirms the lack of impact the last thirty years of *Cahiers* have had: it is still with Bazin and the original teams from the sixties and seventies that the journal's history and identity lies. All those who passed through the offices since the eighties remain dwarfed by the activity and ideas of their predecessors.

164 Frédérique Roussel, '"*Cahiers du cinéma*": clap de reprise', *Libération*, 15 September 2008; Bruno Icher and Frédérique Roussel, 'Gros plan sur les "*Cahiers du cinéma*"', *Libération*, 30 September 2008.

Jean-Pierre and Luc Dardenne, *The Son* (2002)

8

After Cahiers

A journal so deeply embedded in the culture and politics of its times will always to an extent reflect an already-existing, external set of social and political flashpoints in society. A great publication will also step aside and speak against the grain. Historically *Cahiers* has been both representative of its time, and a troublesome presence within it. In the 1980s, *Cahiers* became almost exclusively reflective. Mimicking the broader defeat of the French Left managed by Mitterrand it opted meekly for the consensus that was setting in, the capitulation carried through with such verve by Maoist turncoats under the banner of intransigent realism: 'there is no alternative'. And yet, there were so many battles to be fought, so many critical avenues to go down, so many instances where the difficult, anti-consensual *Cahiers* spirit was absolutely vital to invigorate our engagement with cinema, and naturally through this, with the world.

What *Cahiers* faced in the 1980s was the unprecedented dilemma of having to deal with a film culture and criticism that had fully internalized the *Cahiers* ideas and arguments. The canonization of early Hollywood, the new wave of film-making, the theorization of film criticism and ideological readings: all have had direct impact on the subsequent generations of directors, often highly knowledgeable about movie history and self-conscious successors to the old masters. *Cahiers* needed to deal with a domain that had become, thanks partly to its teachings, fully self-aware. It ducked the challenge, preferring to treat film as a product that could sell magazines.

Did the *Cahiers* story really have to end this way? To present its moves as inevitable, or cast them in broader terms—as the crisis of film criticism—would be wrong. The apocalyptic scenario is easy to invoke.[165] Apart from adding some apparent gravitas to otherwise banal reflections, this view also allows individual projects to explain their failures as part of a broader cultural downturn. While *Cahiers*' shift to the mainstream in the 1980s was closely allied with and influenced by trends in French politics and intellectual culture at the time, this is not the whole story. True, the intellectual life of the country was increasingly played out in the media, as the majority of newspapers, magazines and television channels gravitated towards the neoliberal centre. But *Cahiers* chose to position itself within this world. There were alternatives.

Other traffic

For a time, the leading outrider was Serge Daney. After ten years at *Libération* he felt he had exhausted the possibilities of the journalistic form for criticism; he was tired of playing the paramedic, rushing around to save worthy films from obscurity by performing emergency operations and writing a few lines on them in his column. His hand was also forced by his AIDS diagnosis. So, in 1991, he set in motion a project that had long been in gestation: the launch of his own journal, *Trafic*. 'The few decisions I've made in my life have been negative ones: leaving *Cahiers*, leaving *Libération*. *Trafic* is the only positive one, something of a "last stop, everyone get off here"'.[166]

The first issue appeared in the winter of 1991, a compact 144-page journal without images and a simple brown-paper cover, produced

165 At *Cahiers* it was wheeled out during a roundtable in 1984. Toubiana and Bergala presented a bleak scene in which they were helpless pawns in the face of overwhelming 'mediatic bombardment'. They did accept some responsibility, conceding that as critics they had also failed to rise to the occasion: not writing well enough to 'whet people's appetites'. *Cahiers* 356, May 1984.

166 *Persévérance*, p. 68.

by the small literary publisher POL. *Trafic* too had a strong affiliation with writing: the first issue included an epigraph from Ezra Pound, a poem by Godard and a letter from Rossellini. In its founding statement Daney summarized his long-standing feeling that we now had a more vivid memory of the art of cinema than we did a lived experience of it. Our local screens were no longer hubs for fellow cinephiles, and we were more likely to be moved by a film shown on television. So, a journal of any worth had to tease out the memories by engaging with the questions underlying cinema. To mark its fiftieth issue, *Trafic* published over 600 pages of responses from writers, critics and film-makers to the question 'What is cinema?'

Following Daney's death in 1992, co-editors Raymond Bellour, Jean-Claude Biette, Sylvie Pierre and Patrice Rollet carried on with the project; expanding the editorial committee in 2003, when Biette passed away, to include Leslie Kaplan, Pierre Léon, Jacques Rancière, Jonathan Rosenbaum and Jean-Louis Schefer. Over its nearly seventy issues, the format has altered slightly: the 'letters from' appear more regularly, footnotes are allowed—Daney had been against these, with their whiff of academic pedantry—and the contents are grouped to hint at still unspecified themes.

Trafic provides a space to reflect on cinema outside of market imperatives or academic norms, to consider the back-and-forth traffic of images that have been made over the last century, as well as the movement between media: cinema, television, DVD. It corresponds in this sense to Daney's notion of the critic as *passeur*—a smuggler, border-crosser, go-between for film and its audience—and to the need to write in a way that registers the experience of spectators today, who are discovering cinema just as the art goes through a transition period: its original, explosive and foundational period has passed, but this is still fresh in the memories of older generations who lived through it, and feel its passing as a loss, rather than a rich history.

The ideas pursued by *Trafic* are those *Cahiers* gave up on. Set against the latter's breathless attempts to register everything pertaining to the image, its indiscriminate piggybacking on the latest novelties, *Trafic* is austere. It aspires to 'reposition cinema and cinema alone in a diachronic rather than synchronic history':[167] the old and the new considered as part of the same world. Daney explained:

> It's like a motorway slip road that we suspect actually forms a circle rather than a bend, and will bring us back to where we started from. Consequence: we cannot see ahead, and the one image behind us in the all-embracing thumbnail of the rear-view mirror is constantly changing. Consequence: the pertinence of this little phrase . . . 'as soon as he'd crossed the bridge, the ghosts came to meet him'.[168]

In this description of the critic's standpoint, and the world he inhabits, Daney did not mean ghosts in a malevolent sense, and the glances at the rear-view mirror were not intended to evoke nostalgia. Rather, the metaphors capture *Trafic*'s project as an uncompromisingly historical engagement with film that is not divorced from the present world of cinema. A spirit, in other words, of one step back and two forwards, or *reculer pour mieux sauter*.

Cinephilia's second wind

There are plenty more examples to prove that imaginative, incisive writing on film has not disappeared in France. Bernard Eisenschitz's only recently defunct *Cinéma* offered consistently intelligent insights into the aesthetics and history of cinema in a non-academic format and style.[169] Many issues of the lavishly produced but sparely designed silver booklet also included a DVD of forgotten or previously inaccessible films. Works by John Ford and Kenji Mizoguchi, and Eric Rohmer's documentaries on Stéphane Mallarmé and Victor Hugo, were all made available. Some more strands of vibrant critical activity came together, albeit in loose form, in Adrian Martin and

---

167 *Persévérance*, Paris 1993, p. 158.

168 *Persévérance*, p. 44.

169 The review closed in 2007 after its publisher, Léo Scheer, lost interest and wanted to cut production costs. Eisenschitz refused to compromise, regarding aesthetic design and quality as an extension of the intellectual project.

Jonathan Rosenbaum's book from 2003, *Movie Mutations*, a close collaboration with Raymond Bellour and a handful of other critics around the world.

Most significantly, this was a project, like *Trafic* and *Cinéma*, that was conceived of and executed outside the academy, though without excluding it. The impact of academia on film writing has been mixed: on the one hand greater scholarship on any great director offers potential insights and ensures that the debate on who is included in the canon remains alive. Overlooked masters, lost classics, historical investigations—these subjects are often best pursued in a research environment. On the other hand, the academicization of film writing has allowed for a host of meaningless terms and esoteric vocabulary to be employed: students of film speak one language, everyday film-goers another. Between academics and journalists there is little crossover. One deals with an abstract set of ideas; the other at worst draws judgements based on what he or she saw the week before, and treats the latest Oscars list as the news event of the year.

Movie Mutations contained some spirited polemics against the 'death of cinema and cinephilia' so blithely and frequently announced by even the finest writers, directors and historians. Godard, for example—since his farewell to the movies, *Contempt*, in 1963, up to his exhibition at the Pompidou in 2007—has mourned the death of cinema whilst simultaneously breathing new life into it with every project. Susan Sontag, writing on the 'decay' of the art form in 1995, made the important distinction between the decline of cinema and that of the culture sustaining it. She emphasised the latter. Sontag could not see cinephilia being capable of existing without the old movie theatres of her youth. But, she conceded, 'if you can tolerate the small formats—I happen to have a problem with miniaturized images—you can get the whole history of cinema and watch it over and over again. You don't have to be dependent on the distribution system.' Sontag had hit on one response to the crisis, but saw it as a compromise.[170]

170 Susan Sontag, 'The Decay of Cinema', *New York Times*, 25 February 1996.

The current landscape

In any period, artists and critics face a particular set of challenges unique to their historical conjuncture. The same model cannot be used in a different social and political environment. Neither the original critic-*cinéaste*, nor the radical militant could intervene effectively in today's context. The cultural landscape is very different today. The films of the New Wave served the *coup de grâce* on the conservative fare against which Truffaut and his colleagues polemicized. Today, cinema's role and prominence has been downgraded—and its aesthetic strongly affected—by television, and the ever-greater control by the mass media and advertising corporations over what is shown, where and for how long. A new globalized image regime is now in place, further relativizing all other national film industries with regard to that of America, while mainstream Hollywood is little more than a canning factory for the spectacle. This has produced new poles of opposition and a hard-line approach by critics is necessary. When films are no more than money-spinning repetitions that entrench conventional thought and techniques, critics should say so.

Such changes in the cultural environment are especially evident at festivals. Historically, these had acted as springboards for new talent not always recognized by the industry: Truffaut's success at Cannes with *The 400 Blows*; Buñuel, Fassbinder and Pasolini flowering in Venice and Berlin. But today's directors turn up at Cannes or the Sundance to sell their films in a glamorized cattle market. Festivals have increasingly taken on the same rhythm as the film industry. Whoever wins is assured a secure future as *the* art-house hit of the year, with distributors certain to allocate their one open slot to the successful candidate.[171]

---

171 Miramax offers the best example of this process. The company set up by Harvey and Bob Weinstein in 1979 has very close ties with the Sundance Film Festival. This relationship alone has transformed the interface between art cinema, independent distribution, the multiplexes and mainstream Hollywood, by injecting money as well as cultural cachet into the system. Miramax promotes its own films, and even buys up potential contenders to avoid or control screenings. For a recent anatomy of the industry, see

The main contenders at these showcases for independent film are often as recognizable as the equivalent Oscar movies, following a convergence of aesthetic codes from Hollywood and the avant-garde. Independent films borrow freely from the montage techniques and narrative structures of big-budget releases. In one director's words, 'our survival is not set up by public taste, but by the opinion of our peers—festival programmers, arts-council juries'.[172] What Atom Egoyan has won through escaping box office pressures he has lost in his connection with the public. Given the clout of festivals today, this mirrors the hierarchy in the art world, where 'super-curators' control the circulation and valuation of modern artworks.[173]

A machine-based art

Technological changes have progressively democratized film-making and film-watching, providing a means to be involved with cinema without depending on the terms dictated by major conglomerates. Wider availability of cheap digital video cameras for aspiring directors, and multiregion DVD players for viewers, can subvert market and industry rules, and allow spectators to sidestep strategies of saturation—the designated 'blockbuster' unleashed to fill every screen in town—and the restricted choice dictated by distribution companies. These innovations hold enormous potential for expanding both the practice and understanding of cinema. A narrative of decline would see this as coming at the expense of the craft of directing. Lighter digital cameras and equipment have replaced the manually managed cranes. Many elements that constituted the 'grammar' of

---

Jonathan Rosenbaum, *Movie Wars: How Hollywood and the Media Limit What Movies We Can See*, Chicago 2000.

172 Quoted in Katharine Monk, *Weird Sex and Snowshoes and Other Canadian Film Phenomena*, Vancouver 2002, p. 2. For a breakdown of the festival circuit, see Thomas Elsaesser, *European Cinema: Face to Face with Hollywood*, Amsterdam 2005, pp. 82–107; Marijke de Valck, *Film Festivals*, Amsterdam 2007.

173 See Julian Stallabrass's definitive exposé, *Art Incorporated: The Story of Contemporary Art*, Oxford 2004.

cinematic language have been 'lost': lighting, sound, use of deep focus—just minor details for directors working with a television projection in mind. In any case, most transmitters distort the original size of the film and its intended projection, so that features originally filmed in CinemaScope appear either stretched or compressed on television screens.

Yet film was an art born out of technology. Its craft developed in the meeting between man and machine. The artistry involved in film-making has not disappeared, simply evolved: new practices respond to improved technology. Film-makers are not immobile, bloated ogres barking orders from their chair like the director played by Orson Welles in Pasolini's short *La Ricotta*, about a filming of the crucifixion; they are now manipulating different tools. Digital technology allows the simulations of computer-generated imagery (CGI), but it also liberates the most inventive of artists, enables radical new practices to be pursued, and marginalized issues to receive full attention. This is clear in works such as Wang Bing's documentary of over nine hours, *West of the Tracks* (2003). Given its running time, location and the nature of the project, Wang could only have used a digital camera to record the interviews with workers from the old industrial city of Tiexi, in Shenyang, China. Whatever the impact of viewing film on the small screen, this reality should invigorate critical work: does the art really change before our eyes? If so, how? Should criticism incorporate a more phenomenological element to its interpretations and analyses?

The democratization of film-watching, with the widespread availability of DVD, has exacerbated the decline of cinema audiences and retrospective programmes. Local cine-clubs are a rarity; the norm is for individuals to select their own screenings at home. Can cinephilia really survive in this atomized form? André Labarthe has pointed out that a family fragments at the cinema—in the dark, keeping quiet, behaving in public—more than it does at home, where the television set is part of social space and the same family will watch and experience the film together.[174] There is much truth in this. A

174 Personal communication, January 2009.

genuine encounter with cinema can still happen via a smaller screen; Daney did not survive to witness the arrival of DVD, and had he done so his approach to criticism and to the health of cinema's historical memory would, Jean Douchet believes, have been different.[175] The opportunity to see so many films, to become a cinephile via the small screen is exciting: and if not all generations have the gift of Langlois, his screening programmes remain as a guide. By the same token, critics can and should refer to past classics without worrying that they are talking about an inaccessible world of memories. The art's history continues to live past its first phase of creativity.

Changes in viewing practices have raised the bar for critics. The challenge was not met at *Cahiers*; in the end, it has joined other contemporary writing on cinema that panders to rather than challenges the more atomized situation of today, and does so because it is 'derivative and unclear about its aesthetic commitments'.[176] Hence the banal celebrations of whatever is exotic under the name of 'other' or 'independent' cinema, and the passive, at best symptomatic, readings of Hollywood, as though this were trenchant critique. Negative criticism is rare; the notion of being for or against anything in cinema seems out of place. The rise in film studies departments has, as noted, deepened the isolation of those working in the medium, and conclusively severed the relationship between writing on film and making it.

Bonjour cinéma!

Jean Epstein's excited greeting in the twenties is no less appropriate today. The seventh art continues to present us with startling new aesthetic and narrative forms. In the cinemas of the periphery—Iran, Korea, China, Taiwan—contemporary struggles with the

---

175 Jean Douchet is one critic who has wholeheartedly embraced the new technology, writing reviews in *Cahiers* and elsewhere on DVD releases, taking the disc presentation, extras and transfer quality as a new and discrete subject of criticism in its own right. Douchet's personal 'dvdthèque' forms the content of the first library of the media, currently being set up in Dijon.
176 Peter Wollen, *Paris Hollywood*, p. 232.

contradictions of a belated modernity still find their most powerful expression in film: the work of Abbas Kiarostami, Edward Yang, Jia Zhangke, Hou Hsiao-Hsien. It could be argued that the very monopoly of the new world order over news and current affairs on television is giving rise to countervailing documentary movements, producing work of striking quality in Latin America, China and the Middle East, in which mainstream footage is appropriated and interrogated.

Brazilian José Padilha's *Bus 174* released in 2002 is a formally groundbreaking documentary on the hijacking of a bus in Rio de Janeiro. The dramatic incident had been caught on surveillance camera and broadcast live on television. Padilha combined the found footage and news reporting with commentary from psychologists and interviews with people from the city's *favelas*, as well as the police. His structure presented, first, the material seen by millions watching the news, before taking us inside the bus and into the *favelas* of the hostage-taker. The public's initial support for the police elicited by the original footage was entirely re-evaluated in the light of the new information, and in the process one became able to break down the reactions to the raw, 'spectacular' account and consider how film can challenge these responses. Compared to this, Fernando Meirelles's *City of God* is no more than *favela-chic*, a throwback to the French *look* style with the fast-paced thrills it offers spectators as the camera charges through the Brazilian slums.

In Europe, the political apathy born from decades of managerial politics since the end of the Cold War has been contested by a handful of film-makers. Michael Haneke—both formally and in his subject-matter—has savagely exposed the nature of middle-class conformism and its repressed post-colonial guilt. *Hidden* in 2005 played with its own voyeuristic surveillance perspective to disrupt the complacency, as Haneke sees it, of the viewer as well as the viewed. The 'rewind' moments of his original version of *Funny Games*, by undoing the happy ending, made audiences sit up while accentuating the issue of how violence can be represented on screen in such a way as to retain its brutal horror. In Liège, Belgium, the Dardenne brothers have filmed time and again the same modern-day post-industrial town, with each new work conveying tangible truths on the human condition and showing up the *faux* poverty of Mike Leigh's prettified visions of working-class Britain.

In 2003, Edgar Reitz completed his *Heimat* trilogy, an extraordinarily ambitious attempt to chronicle the modern history of Germany. This *bildungsroman* structure applied to film builds on Fassbinder's penultimate work in 1981, a free adaptation of Alfred Döblin's *Berlin Alexanderplatz*. The very duration of Reitz's project—*Heimat 1* (over 15 hours), *Heimat 2* (over 25 hours) and *Heimat 3* (over 11 hours) transforms the traditional experience of viewing and the possibilities for storytelling. What approach should one take to such a project? What is riding on *how* a viewer experiences the series—whether in chunks at home, in intense sittings at rare cinema screenings, or on television with distinct periods of time between each episode, at the same rhythm as others in the country?

There are directors grappling with all forms of social change, providing images to think with that are qualitatively different from past traditions of film-making. It is in their hands that cinema continues to reinvent itself.

The auteur's bitter victory

As we cast an eye over some of the major works of cinema from recent years, on what basis do we judge these films to be important, and in some cases modern masterpieces? *Cahiers* invented, and compellingly deployed—before embodying and reinventing it in the New Wave—one notion that remains integral to any critical engagement with cinema: the *auteur*. Today, the scattergun use of this term might at first appear to confirm the magazine's long-lasting influence, yet it reveals a bitter victory. The concept itself has been voided of meaning. Directors of all styles and ambitions, operating in any genre—the *cinéma du look* group; the New Wave emulators Assayas, Carax, Desplechin, Téchiné; the populists Claude Berri and Jean-Pierre Jeunet, and in America Quentin Tarantino, Michael Mann, the Coen brothers—all either use the title as a self-description, or have it pressed upon them by critics. There is such a thing as 'doing auteurism', especially in France, where one must claim this title before even making a film so as to be eligible for funding. As the film historian René Prédal noted, there is a real 'leniency' around the notion compared to the 'strictness' of the *politique*: rather than the privileged few selected by François Truffaut, 'auteurism is now a convenient label'.[177]

Cahiers did not disagree with Prédal's verdict. In practice, however, what the magazine condemned on one page it fuelled anew on the next by consecrating the likes of Assayas or Carax after just one film, or treating as serious artists Hollywood's movie brats. In the rush to cover as much as possible, be *dans le vent*, or 'with-it', *Cahiers* opened its doors to every pretender. Looking back at their designated 'top films' and major 'events' during the eighties and nineties, few choices proved historic. Téchiné's *Scene of the Crime*, Bertrand Blier's *Merci la vie*, Desplechin's *La Sentinelle*, Carax's *The Lovers on the Bridge*: all these films seem to indulge in a pointless mixture of genres and aesthetics, with little interest in pursuing one subject with any depth.[178] The first works by Desplechin and Assayas, for example, convey an unsatisfying mixture of strangeness and banality at once. Their films are conceptually driven vehicles for some navel-gazing protagonists, isolated from their environment by the camera's own indifference to showing the world in which they exist.[179]

---

177 René Prédal, *Le Cinéma d'auteur. Une vieille lune?*, Paris 2001, p. 130.

178 In 1991 a real fetishism of the *auteur* was displayed when *Cahiers* 448 was dedicated entirely to Carax's film. The pages reproduced scraps of text, scribbled notes and photos from the set.

179 Thierry Jousse did write a damning review of Blier's *Merci la vie*, detecting a 'musty whiff of modernity' in the film-in-a-film conceit. Blier edited according to the channel-hopper's rule book, but for all its action the film was full of corpses. It had a 'deadly movement that sticks to the skin and prevents the film from going forwards. Can we still make cinema with so little flesh and blood? I don't know. But what I do know is that in *Merci la vie*, life, and therefore cinema, clears off'. *Cahiers* 442, April 1991. Jousse was the chief editor at the time, but his severe verdict did not determine the magazine's general coverage of the film. Jousse's review was hidden away in a small column in a later issue, after *Merci la vie* had made *Cahiers*' front cover and was designated 'Film of the Month'. Blier enjoyed a cosy interview with

The magnificent endurance of Samuel Fuller might be remembered here, now that directors barely out of film school are being admitted to the canon. As Fuller shows, to be an *auteur* you must earn your stripes; many wars later, if you are still standing, then perhaps the nomination to be included among the elite of masters may come. Until then: work, offer and develop your world view, but that's it. While the term also conveys a particular way of conceiving cinema, a belief in its singularity as an art, simply thinking of oneself as an *auteur* is not enough. Yet this became a main factor in *Cahiers*' celebration of French directors who made their first films in the eighties and nineties. High praise was dished out to any who defended the practice of artistic film-making, as though the discourse were somehow performative, and relieved them of the need to actually advance the art through the films they made.

Heeding Bazin

Bazin advocated a specifically dialectical exchange between critic and director, and exemplified this in his engagement with Jean Renoir's work. The *politique* lent itself too readily to personality cults. It undermined the role of the critic in explaining the oeuvre both to the audience and to directors themselves. Bazin had no wish to be a mere generator of eulogies; he was wary of submitting to one creator's superior genius. Rather, he believed the critic could develop a close relationship with the practising artist. This model retains the notion of *auteur*, but allows for the possibility of a critic being better placed to detect the operations behind the work, something its author might not be capable of formulating so lucidly. As Renoir himself admitted, it was only after reading Bazin's texts on his films that he really understood what he had been doing, and what the works were actually about.

The arguments the *politique* ignited also drew out the always tense

Toubiana, whose own opinion was quite the opposite to Jousse's: 'I don't know whether *Merci la vie* is Blier's most accomplished film at the formal level, but it is without doubt his most sincere, most daring and in particular, his most alive'. *Cahiers* 441, March 1991.

relationship between content and form. *Mise en scène* was a vital notion that allowed critics to engage with a film more completely: a care for the cinematic presentation encouraged a way of watching that concentrated on how narrative was expressed through form. In its eagerness to defend a particular director, however, the *politique* could all too easily ignore the quality of the narrative. From the start, in other words, the *auteur* concept was richly ambiguous: how far is the director conscious of his creative individuality? Does the *politique* subject the critic to the psychology of the director alone, granting too much significance to conscious intention without attending closely enough to narrative, especially when dealing with genre cinema? Does the *politique* exclude the possibility of judging individual failures by its blanket acceptance of what Renoir said about his own work—that the director is only ever making one film?

The tension between content and form is an issue for all critics. *Cahiers'* history shows some of the directions an exploration of that relationship can take: from the controversial *politique* to the structuralism and semiotics that located the source of meaning in the subconscious landscape of a director's mind, manifested through his films in a symbolic form which the critic's task is to decode. In the eighties, *Cahiers* based its reorientation to some extent around a purported 'return to narrative', and yet it retained just a small part of the way this operates in film—description, theme—and put aside the exploration of a specifically visual language. New Hollywood could thus legitimately return to the magazine via an analysis that often elevated the quality of its productions by intellectually exploring them, while ignoring their total formal redundancy. At ever higher costs and in increasingly computer-generated forms, the blockbuster should today be a main target for critical attack, exposing the majority of these works as corporate commodities, formulaic and passively spectacular. (As it is, dismayingly, we must look to the Orange mobile phone ads to perform this essential function.)

Cahiers' 'American turn' paradoxically served to block out much of the radical writing on film that was being produced in the United States during the 1980s and 1990s. Fredric Jameson's 1992 *The Geopolitical Aesthetic*, for example, provided landmark comparative readings of Edward Yang's *Terrorizer*, Sokurov's *Days of Eclipse*, Godard's *Passion* and sundry American paranoid conspiracy movies, within a global context of complex cultural and political inequalities. During the same period, Roberto Schwarz was writing to powerful effect on the experience of military dictatorship in Brazil, exemplified in the *mise en scène* of Eduardo Coutinho's *A Man Marked Out to Die*.

Today our understanding of film has entered the modernist phase. Artistic self-awareness on the part of film-makers is taken for granted in the twenty-first century, so much so that it has generated a genre, with recognizable tics, topics and structures. Tarantino's films are even a parody of this, as indeed was Assayas's tiresome and pointless *Irma Vep* from 1996. Whatever critical positions *Cahiers* still takes against some directors and movements are tokenistic, because it implicitly accepts the existence of a generic *auteur* cinema that needs neither justification nor reprimand.

These snapshots of the challenges, changes, bright hopes and dangers that exist in the contemporary culture of film and its active production painfully accentuate *Cahiers'* absence as a pioneering commentator. When it ceased to base its critical engagement with film around a set of independent, aesthetic ideas, the project fell apart. Today the magazine limps on, defended by many—as the signed letter from old editors and friends in April 2008 makes clear—but the still lively and sympathetic spirit that informs its discussion and defence of cinema is expressed in the broadest of terms, as the dedication to serious thinking and writing on film outside the academy. Even this diminished ambition, *Cahiers* now only represents in name.

John Huston, *The Misfits* (1961)

Afterword

What lessons can we draw from *Cahiers*' history? Its successive generations of editors brought distinctive developments in both outlook and agenda—philosophy or the barricades; aestheticism or channel-hopping—yet they always retained the sense of being in the cinematic vanguard, as passionate as they were interventionist. The collapse of such a project could be the cue for apocalyptic judgements on the art, and on the practice of film criticism more generally. When editors at *Cahiers* adopted such an explanation for their own sense of impotence in the face of a culture saturated with images, it simply provided a rationale for their reorientation to the centre. According to this analysis, a magazine either perishes with its ideals or it gets real, reconnects with the changed world and accepts its terms. The only way to survive is to chase after anything that is new in the hope of remaining relevant. As this history has shown, such 'realism' is a fraud: once equipped with a set of clear and passionate convictions a film magazine will run for as long as these are sustained, defended and challenged. In the eighties *Cahiers* lost its belief in both the radical project and the capacity of the public to engage with serious ideas about cinema. It gave up its aspiration to make history.

If there are films to be loved and championed, films you believe in and that teach you about life as well as about how to film life, you pick up your *stylo-caméra* and write about them. You do not trouble yourself with what the market or public thinks it wants: states of mind, obstinate and conservative views can be transformed if you show, through writing, the nature of films passing on the screen.

The archive that *Cahiers* has left behind is a vivid reminder of all that can be achieved when film is lived and breathed by those who write on it, when writing on film and making film are like a single arc. Today there are new film-makers to explore, new works to tackle and always the old masters to meet afresh with every viewing. The seventh art is young. *Cahiers* may now be a dead sun, but it has left us with one of the richest sources for understanding both cinema's past and its future. In the ashes of *Cahiers du cinéma*, a thousand phoenix can be reborn.

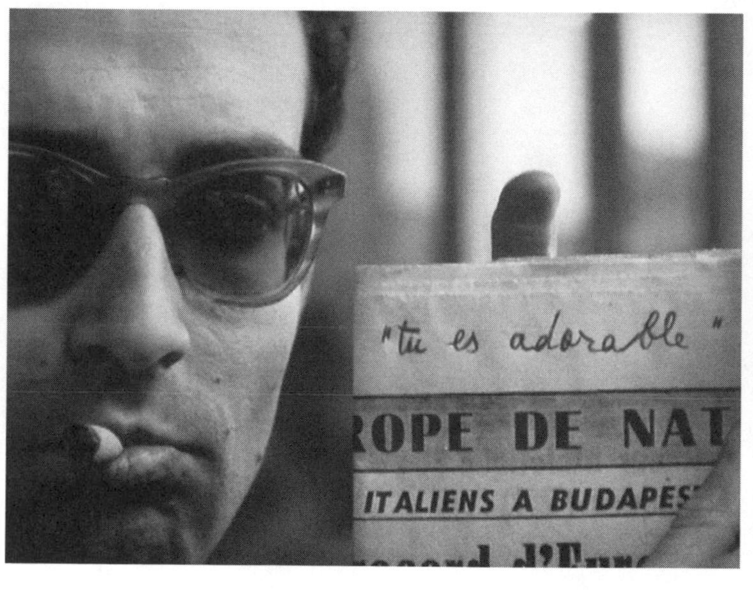

Jacques Rivette, *Paris Belongs To Us* (1960)

Index

Page numbers in *italics* indicate photographs